Introduction To DATABASE SYSTEMS

Stéphane Bressan

Barbara Catania

McGraw Hill

Singapore • Boston • Burr Ridge, IL • Dubuque, IA • Madison, WI • New York • San Francisco
St. Louis • Bangkok • Bogotá • Caracas • Kuala Lumpur • Lisbon • London • Madrid
Mexico City • Milan • Montreal • New Delhi • Santiago • Seoul • Sydney • Taipei • Toronto

The McGraw·Hill Companies

Introduction to Database Systems

McGraw Hill Education

Copyright © 2005 by McGraw-Hill Education (Asia). All rights reserved. No part of this publication may be reproduced or distributed in any form or by any means, or stored in a data base or retrieval system, without the prior written permission of the publisher.

3 4 5 6 7 8 9 10 ANL 09 08 07 06

When ordering this title, use ISBN 007-124650-9

Printed in Singapore

Contents

Preface		**vii**
About the Authors		**ix**
1	**What's in a Database?**	**1**
1.1	What's in a Database Application?	1
1.2	What's in a Database Management System?	3
2	**Relational Model**	**9**
2.1	The Relational Model	9
2.2	Integrity Constraints	14
3	**Relational Calculus**	**19**
3.1	Logic and Calculus	19
3.2	T-uple Relational Calculus (TRC)	20
	3.2.1 The Syntax of TRC	20
	3.2.2 The Semantics of TRC	23
	3.2.3 Queries in TRC	26
3.3	Domain Relational Calculus (DRC)	28
	3.3.1 The Syntax of DRC	28
	3.3.2 The Semantics of DRC	30
	3.3.3 Queries in DRC	33
3.4	Safety	34
4	**Relational Algebra**	**37**
4.1	Operators and Composability	37
4.2	Standard Sct Operators	37
4.3	Operators Involving the Structure of Relations	41
4.4	Queries	46
4.5	The Myth of Declarativeness	48

5 SQL   51
5.1 A Standard 51
5.2 Data Definition Language 52
5.3 Data Manipulation Language 60
    5.3.1 Updates 60
    5.3.2 Simple Queries 62
    5.3.3 Aggregate Queries 67
    5.3.4 Nested Queries 69

6 SQL and Programming Languages   73
6.1 Motivation 73
6.2 Procedural SQL 77
    6.2.1 Manipulation 78
    6.2.2 Transactions and Exception Handling 82
    6.2.3 Stored Procedures and Functions 83
    6.2.4 Example 85
6.3 Database Connectivity 86
    6.3.1 The Database Connectivity Reference Architecture . . 87
    6.3.2 Connection 89
    6.3.3 Manipulation 90
    6.3.4 Transactions and Exception Handling 95
    6.3.5 Example 95
6.4 Embedded SQL 97
    6.4.1 Reference Architecture 97
    6.4.2 Connection 98
    6.4.3 Manipulation 98
    6.4.4 Transactions and Exception Handling 101
    6.4.5 Example 101

7 Entity-Relationship Model   105
7.1 Entities and Relationships 105
7.2 Constraints 110
    7.2.1 Implicit and Explicit Constraints 110
    7.2.2 Identity 111
    7.2.3 Participation 113

		7.2.4	Weak Entities	114
	7.3	Mapping ER Diagrams to Relational Schemas	117

8 Normalisation   123
   8.1 Anomalies and Decomposition 123
       8.1.1 Anomalies 123
       8.1.2 Lossless Decomposition 125
       8.1.3 Dependency Preserving Decomposition 128
       8.1.4 Too Much Decomposition Harms 128
   8.2 Functional Dependencies 130
       8.2.1 Keys 131
       8.2.2 Reasoning about Functional Dependencies 133
       8.2.3 Dependency Preserving Decomposition 140
   8.3 Normalisation 141

9 Conclusion   147
   9.1 Further Readings 147

References   151

Index   153

Preface

"He referred to it sardonically and with secret pride as the 'little book,' always giving the word 'little' a special twist, as though he were putting a spin on a ball."

E.B. White, introduction to the 1979 edition of the *The Elements of Style* by W. Strunk Jr. and E.B. White

What's in a Database Course? To some extent it is questionable whether the study of databases should constitute an independent module or even a topic in a higher education computer science curriculum. Indeed, the design, implementation and maintenance of a database application involve all aspects of computer science, from design and modelling, human computer interface, networking, data structures and algorithms, to even hardware. From this viewpoint, a database application is just another computer application. Yet, there are a number of requirements that are specific to a database application to the point that they characterise it and that they justify our study of the principles underlying the management of data and of the principles of the systems that have been designed and implemented for such a task: database management systems.

What's in a Database Textbook? The motivation behind this book is the concise presentation of the main and fundamental concepts underlying database modelling and database querying. We present the basic concepts and the standard tools for the design and for the implementation, in particular querying, of a database application using a database management system. We focus on relational technology for it is today's most established database technology. We generally ignore the issues related to the tuning of applications, which require a deeper understanding of the architecture, algorithms and data structures that are the core of database management systems.

For the sake of rigour, we have decided to introduce t-uple and domain relational calculus before relational algebra. The two topics are covered in

Chapter 3. Relational algebra is discussed in a separate chapter, Chapter 4, in which the definitions of the operators are explicitly given as queries in t-uple relational calculus. This order of presentation may be confusing to some readers. It is possible, however, to read Chapter 4 before proceeding to Chapter 3 for a more intuitive approach.

We have also decided to include a chapter introducing contemporary approaches to coupling SQL and programming languages. This chapter aims at complementing the chapter on SQL and at enabling the practical understanding of the concepts presented elsewhere in the book. This chapter constitutes neither a platform's documentation nor a complete programming guide. It uses concrete examples to illustrate the various aspects of the possible, however, coupling approaches in a concrete syntax. The reader interested in developing an application using one of this approaches needs to refer to user manuals and other proper documentations for further details.

The book is organised as follows. In the first chapter, we identify the specific requirements of a database application. We also show how these requirements are met by the database management systems used to implement and manage database applications. In Chapter 2 we introduce the relational model. Then we present t-uple and domain relational calculus in Chapter 3. Chapter 4 is on relational algebra. Armed with knowledge of the three theoretical query languages for the relational model, in Chapter 5, we study the concrete query language used by most database management systems: SQL. Chapter 6 presents various mainstream approaches to coupling a programming language and SQL. In Chapter 7 we cover the Entity-Relationship model and the Entity-Relationship diagrams for the conceptual design of a database application. Chapter 8 discusses the techniques used to transform relational schemas in order to prevent design anomalies. We conclude with a brief catalogue raisonné of the textbooks that we suggest to accompany this text.

Note: The pronoun 'she' used in this book refers to both genders.

About the Authors

Dr. Stéphane Bressan is Senior Lecturer in the Computer Science department of the School of Computing at the National University of Singapore and Adjunct Associate Professor in the Information Technology department of the Malaysia University of Science and Technology. In 1987, he graduated from *Ecole Universitaire des Ingénieurs de Lille*, France, in Electrical Engineering. He received his Ph.D. in Computer Science from the University of Lille, France, in 1992. From 1990 to 1996 he worked as Researcher at the European Computer-industry Research Centre of Bull, ICL, and Siemens in Munich, Germany. From 1996 to 1998, he was Research Associate at the Sloan School of Management of the Massachusetts Institute of Technology in Cambridge, Massachusetts, United States of America. He is co-editor and co-author of several books including *XML Data Management: Native XML and XML-Enabled Database Systems*(2003).

Dr. Barbara Catania is Associate Professor at the department of Computer and Information Sciences of the University of Genoa, Italy. In 1993, she graduated from the University of Genoa, Italy, in Information Sciences. She received her Ph.D. in Computer Science from the University of Milan, Italy, in 1998. She has been Visiting Researcher at the European Computer-industry Research Centre of Bull, ICL, and Siemens in Munich, Germany, and at the National University of Singapore. She is co-editor and co-author of several books including *Indexing Techniques for Advanced Database Systems*(1997), *Intelligent Database Systems*(2001) and *Sistemi di Basi di Dati – Concetti e Architetture* (in Italian, 1997).

Chapter 1

What's in a Database?

"Sans la raison, la mémoire est incomplète et inefficace."[1]

G. Bachelard, *la dialectique de la durée*

1.1 What's in a Database Application?

If we define a database application as an application that manages data, we have probably embraced in such a definition most, if not all, computer applications. We need a more refined definition that captures everyone's idea that a database application has to do with large amounts of data, big capacity disks, server computers and many users. The requirements characterising and defining a database application may come to mind in different order and may seem to have varying degrees of importance, depending on one's own experience.

The first requirement that we will discuss is related to this not so unfounded idea that databases have to do with secondary storage. First, it seems reasonable to consider that an application dealing with data has among its important requirements that of *persistence*: "thou shall keep my data". Persistence is the property of data (or more precisely of the memory that holds the data) to survive the process that created the data. As a consequence, the data can be re-used by and shared with other processes. Main memory is volatile. If the computer is shut down, even in normal technological conditions, data in main memory is likely to be lost or at least seriously corrupted. Secondary memory, e.g. magnetic disk, and tertiary memory, e.g. tape, are persistent.

When an application needs to manipulate *large amounts of data*, i.e., amounts of data that may not fit at once into main memory of a standard

---

[1]Without 'reason', memory is incomplete and inefficient.

computer, then the developers are confronted with the issue of finding a compromise between the cost and the speed of memory they use, since, in the current state of technology, the cost of memory is commensurate with the speed of access it provides. When data are kept in secondary or tertiary storage, one needs to devise efficient algorithms taking into account the dominant cost of input and output operations, i.e., the transfer between these memories and the main memory of the computer. Such algorithms are called external algorithms. A typical example of an external algorithm is *external sort*, which is used to sort more data than the main memory of a given computer can host at once.

Fortunately, it is often the case that an application that needs to manage large amounts of data, in practice, often needs to manipulate collections of similar objects, i.e., *homogeneous collections*. We can then hopefully predict access patterns and devise indexing and access methods for efficient storage and retrieval.

Furthermore, for most applications, data in the homogeneous collections are *structured*. Typically, traditional database applications manipulate data that can be represented in the form of records. Following this observation, researchers and engineers have devised data models to facilitate the design of applications around the data. Together with the data models, they have devised definition and manipulation languages to describe, create, update and retrieve data. Advanced data models also allow the definition of *integrity constraints* that capture the application's business rules.

Users and applications often access data over a network, possibly at the same time. The access to data and processing capabilities must be *distributed* and possibly *concurrent*. In order to guarantee the integrity of the data in spite of the concurrent access and the possible failures of the programs, systems and media, one needs to devise *concurrency control* and *recovery* strategies. These strategies are based on the notion of *transaction*. A transaction is a logical unit of work carried out by a user or an application: a set of operations. It is wish-able to guarantee *ACID* properties of the transaction for sound concurrency control and recovery: *Atomicity, Consistency, Isolation* and *Durability*. Atomicity guarantees that transactions are either committed (all changes are effective) or aborted and rolled back (all changes are undone, for instance, if integrity constraints are violated or if the transaction is interrupted by a failure and cannot terminate). Durability is synonym to persistence of the effect of committed transactions. Isolation guarantees that concurrent transactions can be understood independently one from another. Consistency guarantees that the net effect of individual transactions leaves the database in a consistent state.

Finally, in most applications it is necessary to control the *access rights* to the data. Indeed, different users and programs may have different rights to define, create, update, delete or query the data.

We therefore propose the following definition of a database application.

> *A database application manages homogeneous collections of large amounts of persistent and structured data that are shared among distributed users and processes and whose integrity must be maintained and security controlled.*

Typical database applications are found in domains such as banking, airline ticket reservation, enterprise resource planning, on-line e-shops and personal data management. It is not necessary for an application to compel all the requirements mentioned above to qualify as a database application. For instance, the electronic management of a personal address book is probably not concerned with large amounts of shared data. Yet, it can be designed using tools for the development and management of a database application and it can benefit by the modelling and querying facilities as well as by the recovery features, for instance. Similarly, although most modern database applications need to manipulate unstructured or semi-structured data such as multimedia data, free text or marked-up text, they can leverage the traditional database technology.

1.2 What's in a Database Management System?

A database application is usually implemented and managed using a *database management system* or *DBMS* for short. A database management system is a collection of software that facilitates the implementation and management of database applications. The database management system implements generic algorithms and offers general tools. It provides support for the fulfilment of the requirements that we have discussed in the previous section.

The life cycle of a database application is complex since it does not only encompass the analysis, design, development, testing and deployment phases, but also a continuous management and upgrading phase since the data managed are often critical to the enterprise running the application. The sublanguages available to implement and manage a database application can be classified into three categories: *the data definition language (DDL)*, the *data manipulation language (DML)* and the *database control language (DCL)*. The users of a database management system are numerous and different. The designers and programmers design and program the application using the tools and languages, DDL and DML, available with the database management system. The database administrator manages the daily services authorising users, programming back-ups and tuning the application over time using mainly the DCL. To this extent it is preferable that the administrator be involved in the design and implementation phase since she may need to modify the application. End-users interact with the database application hosted by the database management system through interface programs. They need not be aware of the underlying programs and of the database management system.

Conventionally, the hardware used by a database management system involves a main computer, the server, attached to large disks and connected through the network to clients from which data and services are accessed. Today's solutions may involve a distributed network of computer servers, clients and disks and the future may see peer-to-peer database management systems architectures.

The database management system lies between the physical storage of data on hardware and the users. Figure 1.1 outlines the main components of a database management system.

The statements in the DDL, DML and DCL are processed and optimised by the *query optimiser*. The *query evaluation engine* forwards them to the underlying *storage manager* for processing and their results are returned to it for presentation to the users and programs. The interface of the storage manager is the *file and access methods manager*, which is in terms of files

Section 1.2. What's in a Database Management System? 5

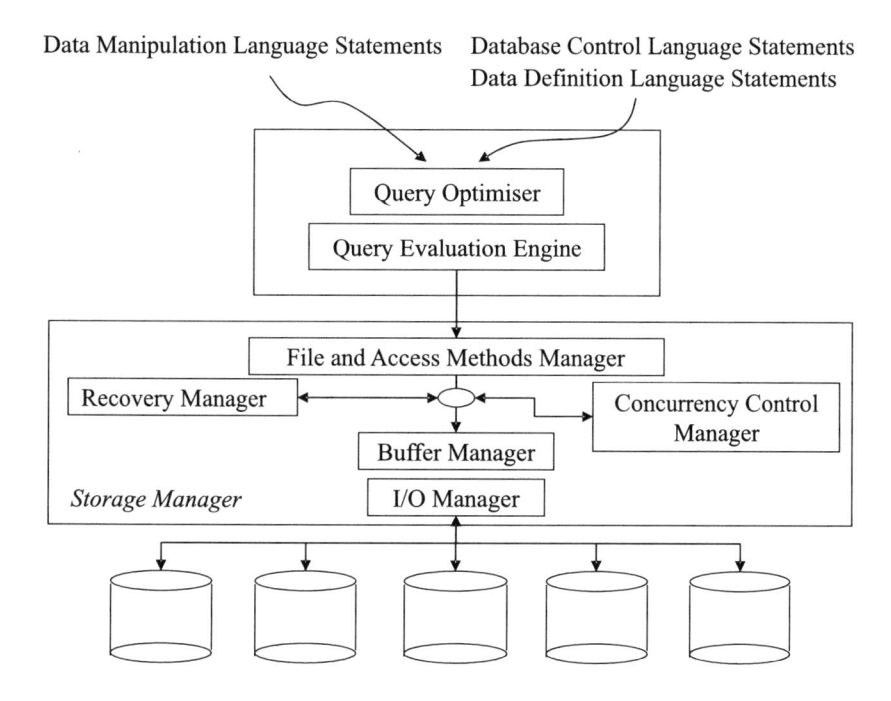

Figure 1.1: Architecture of a DBMS

and access structures such as indices. The file and access methods manager interacts with the storage through a buffer in the main memory of the server. The *buffer manager* brings the data to main memory, calling the *input-output manager*, which drives the storage devices (disks, tapes and CD-ROMs for instance). Interactions between the file and access methods manager and the buffer manager are controlled and monitored by the *recovery manager* and the *concurrency control manager*.

Consequently, as illustrated in Figure 1.2, the data stored and managed by the database management system consist not only of the application data but also of numerous meta- and ancillary data such as log data for recovery, indices for efficient access, rights for access control, dictionary containing data definitions and statistics for optimisation.

Of course, designing a database application consists of choosing a repre-

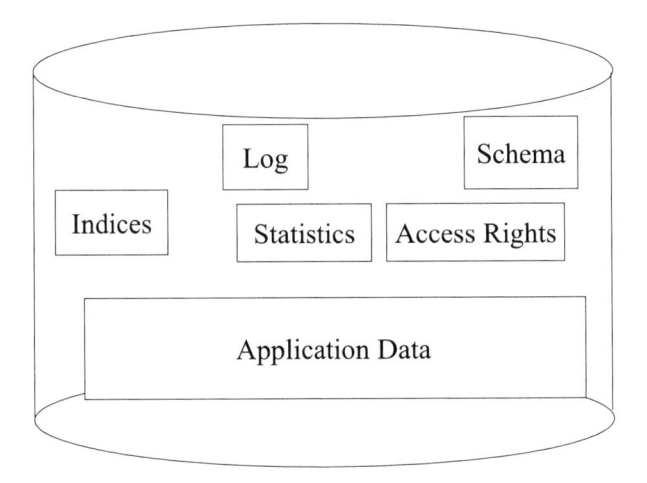

Figure 1.2: Persistent Data Managed by a DBMS

sentation for data. At the lowest level, this means making a decision about the data structures to be used to store the data on disk and to manipulate them in main memory. But this level is managed generically by the database management system. The hierarchy of software components composing the database management system has been designed to free the programmers and the administrator from the details of the *physical data model*. They program and manage the database application in terms of a *logical data model* and *query language* implemented by the database management system rather than in terms of direct and procedural access to data on the hardware devices or even in terms of files and proprietary data structures. This notion of abstraction from the physical model by a logical model is called *physical data independence*. Rich logical data models and their languages also provide tools that offer different users and different programmers customised views of the data in the application. In an enterprise resource planning system, for instance, the accounting department manipulates the data in the database in an appropriate and filtered representation, while the human resource department manipulates a different, also customised, representation. This property is called *logical data independence*. These ideas are illustrated

Section 1.2. What's in a Database Management System?   7

in Figure 1.3 representing the standard three tiers architecture of a database application as defined by the Codasyl and ANSI/X3/SPARC committees in the 1970's. Modern data models and languages also offer a level of *knowledge independence* by allowing the programmers to express and share business rules, views, procedures and triggers that are managed and enforced by the database management system.

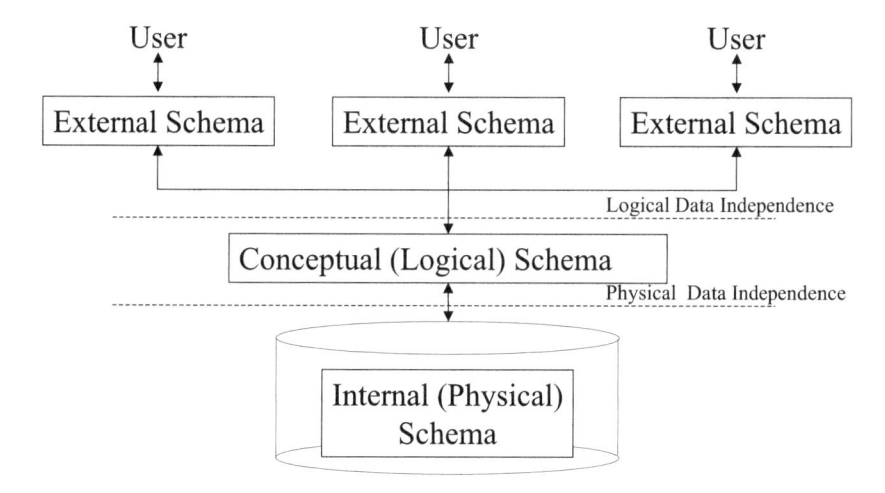

Figure 1.3: ANSI/X3/SPARC Standard Architecture of a Database Application

At the first stage of the design process, the designers use a *conceptual model* to capture the real world entities of interest and map them to the logical model. Of course, the designers, programmers and administrator, given their knowledge of the typical or expected workload of the application, may give some hints about the best way to arrange data at the physical level. They may suggest the use of indices, replication and partitioning of the data, for instance. Such a refinement of the implementation at the physical level is called *database tuning*.

Historically, data models have moved from more physical models to more conceptual models. In other words, the degree of physical data independence has increased. Early data models such as the hierarchical model or the network model constrained the programmers to a view of the data that is too close to the actual implementation. These models and the systems that support them are still used to develop applications in which efficiency and tuning is a major issue, provided their weaknesses do not become obstacles to the realisation of the application itself. The relational model is a logical data model. It is the model implemented by most modern database management systems. Its main query language, Structured Query Language (SQL), is standardised. New logical models such as object-oriented models try to offer richer, more conceptual notions such as objects, encapsulation, object identity or inheritance. Yet these models and the database management systems that implement them are not as mature as the relational database management system technology, which is the result of years of research and development, and deployment. The popular object-relational models of most current database management systems try to combine the robustness of relational technology with the conceptual features of object-oriented models and languages in a single system. The latest version of SQL, SQL-99, the *ANSI/ISO/IEC 9075* 1999 standard, already embeds some object-oriented constructs. This combination is promising. It is likely to become the standard for most future database applications.

We focus in this book on the relational model and relational query languages for they are the basic of today's database technology.

Chapter 2
Relational Model

2.1 The Relational Model

The relational model is a logical data model. E. F. Codd first presented it in 1970 in the seminal article "A Relational Model for Large Shared Data Banks" (see Stonebraker and Hellerstein, 1998).

The relational model leverages a simple mathematical notion, the *relation*, to describe and represent records and homogeneous collections of records. Consequently, the model is formally defined, its properties explained and proven, and formal query languages, such as t-uple calculus or domain relational calculus, defined. The model is very simple since it uses a single data structure, the relation, and its implementation counterpart, the table. Yet it seems powerful enough to be able to naturally represent data for a large variety of applications. Similarly, it leads to expressive yet simple concrete query languages such as SQL.

Figure 2.1 shows the tabular form of a relation used to represent data in a corporate application. The relation or table stores information about departments of a company: the name of a department, its location, the name of the department's manager and the budget of the department.

department_name	location	manager	budget
accounting	107 Jurong Road	Paul Smith	1000000
human resource	10 Western Plaza	Jeremy Sentoso	900000
marketing	107 Jurong Road	Emilda Ramakuti	400000
operations	10 Western Plaza	Emy Laurent	1500000
sales	107 Jurong Road	Peter Ho	2000000

Figure 2.1: Instance of the *department* Relation

Let us now define the elements of the relational model.

Definition 2.1 *We call domain a set of values.*

Examples of domains are the set of integers, the set {"Monday", Tuesday", "Wednesday", "Thursday", "Friday", "Saturday", "Sunday"}, the set of Booleans, the set of dates, the set of strings of length n or less etc. In this book, we restrict ourselves to domains of atomic or scalar values. We exclude domains that are sets of complex objects such as sets of sets, sets of lists and relations. Relations whose domains are only constituted of atomic values are said to be in first normal form or 1NF. There exist data models that allow domains of complex objects. They are usually called complex object models (not to be confused with object-oriented data models, which primarily introduce a notion of object identity) or nested relational models. Relations using such domains are in non first normal form or NF^2 (not to be confused with the second normal form or 2NF, confer Chapter 8).

Definition 2.2 *A relation scheme R is a list of attributes $[A_1, A_2, \cdots, A_n]$ and a list of domains $[D_1, D_2, \cdots, D_n]$. The attributes are distinct. Each attribute is associated with a domain. We denote the relation scheme*

$$R(A_1 : D_1, A_2 : D_2, \cdots, A_n : D_n)$$

or simply

$$R(A_1, A_2, \cdots, A_n)$$

if we need not consider the domains.

For instance, the relation *department* has the following relation scheme where $VARCHAR(24)$, $VARCHAR(36)$ and $NUMERIC$ are domains of strings of characters of variable length and maximum length 24 and 36, and of numbers, respectively.

$$\begin{aligned} department(\quad & department\_name : VARCHAR(24), \\ & location : VARCHAR(36), \\ & manager : VARCHAR(24), \\ & budget : NUMERIC) \end{aligned}$$

Since the attributes are distinct, i.e., they have different names, it is possible to define the relation scheme as a set of attributes (instead of a list), each of which is associated with a domain. Yet by defining the scheme of a relation as list we can reference attributes by their position. We often ignore the domains and represent a relation scheme as, for example, follows:

$$department(department\_name, location, manager, budget).$$

The number of attributes in a relation scheme is called the *degree* or *arity* of the relation. The relation *department* whose instance is illustrated in Figure 2.1 has degree 4. It can also be said that it has arity 4.

Definition 2.3 *A relation instance, noted* $[R]$, *of the relation scheme* $R(A_1 : D_1, A_2 : D_2, \cdots, A_n : D_n)$ *is a subset of the Cartesian product* $D1 \times D_2 \times \cdots \times D_n$. *Elements of* $[R]$ *are called t-uples.* $Dom(A)$ *to denote the domain associated with attribute* A.

A relation instance is therefore a set of t-uples. Figure 2.1 represents an instance of the relation *department*. The number of t-uples in a relation instance is called the *cardinality* of the relation instance. The instance of the relation department illustrated in Figure 2.1 has cardinality 5. It would be mathematically appropriate to simply call a relation instance a relation. Some authors do so while others call relation the relation scheme. We shall freely use the term 'relation' to refer to a relation scheme or to a relation instance whenever it is not ambiguous.

Definition 2.4 *A relational database schema is a set of relation schemes.*

Let us, for instance, consider the schema of an application involving employees and departments of a company. Employees have a name and an address. Employees work for departments of the company. Employees joined a department at a given date. Departments have a name, a location, a manager, who is an employee herself, and a budget. The schema of the database could comprise three relations, *employee*, *work_for* and *department* with the following schemes, respectively.

$$\begin{aligned}employee(\quad & employee\_name : VARCHAR(24),\\ & address : VARCHAR(36))\end{aligned}$$

work_for(*employee_name* : $VARCHAR(24)$,
                department_name : $VARCHAR(24)$,
                date : $DATE$)

department(*department_name* : $VARCHAR(24)$,
                location : $VARCHAR(36)$,
                manager : $VARCHAR(24)$,
                budget : $NUMERIC$)

The instances of the three relations are represented in Figure 2.1 for the *department* relation, Figure 2.2 for the *work_for* relation and Figure 2.3 for the *employee* relation.

employee_name	department_name	date
Emy Laurent	operations	12/02/2001
Jain Singh	human resource	02/02/2001
Jeremy Sentoso	human resource	04/03/2001
John McMallen	sales	06/12/2001
Kwok Li Shin	sales	11/12/2001
Nancy Santi	human resource	03/03/2001
Nancy Santi	sales	01/04/2001
Paul Smith	accounting	07/05/2001
Peter Ho	operations	12/12/2001
Peter Ho	sales	01/11/2003
Putri Bte Mohamed	accounting	04/03/2002
Reza Ernawati	accounting	06/02/2001
Yao Chen	sales	11/11/2001
Zhou Li	operations	08/05/2002

Figure 2.2: Instance of the *work_for* Relation

Section 2.1. The Relational Model

employee_name	address
Emilda Ramakuti	101 East Coast Crescent
Emy Laurent	107 Jurong Road
Jain Singh	10 Johor Way
Jeremy Sentoso	107 Jurong Road
John McMallen	107 Jln Kampung Baru
Kwok Li Shin	19 Johor Way
Nancy Santi	123 Pantai Street
Paul Smith	22 Bukit Ridge
Peter Ho	22 Bukit Ridge
Putri Bte Mohamed	12 Raffles Road
Reza Ernawati	19 Johor Way
Wang Chee Leong	100 Centre Point
Yao Chen	123 Pantai Street
Zhou Li	19 Bencoolen Lane

Figure 2.3: Instance of the *employee* Relation

Definition 2.5 *The set of relation instances of a relational database schema is called the instance of the schema or state of the database. Sometimes it is simply referred to as the database.*

In addition to normal values, each domain contains a special value called the null value. In variants of the relational model and in different systems, null values may have several different meanings. Indeed, a null value could indicate that the value of the attribute for which it is used is not known, does not exist, or both (it is not even known whether the value of the attribute is not known or does not exist). For instance, the null value in the following t-uple[1] may indicate that we do not know the address of Ng Wee Hyong.

$employee('Ng\ Wee\ Hyong', null)$

---
[1] We use single quotes for strings in compliance with the SQL standard.

The null value in the following t-uple may indicate that the training department does not have a manager.

$department('training', '110\ Jln\ Lempeng', null, 120000)$

The precise semantics of null values should be clearly understood before null values are used. In particular, we need to carefully think about their behaviour in queries. How can we answer a query looking for employees living in Jurong since we do not know whether Mr. Ng does or does not live there? Can we declare that two departments have the same manager if they both have no manager? Readers can refer to textbooks mentioned in Chapter 9 to find out more about the theoretical and practical issues related to null values. In general, unless explicitly indicated, the reader should assume that we do not consider null values.

2.2 Integrity Constraints

Some readers may wonder why we did not choose a different schema for the database application described in the previous section. Indeed, we could use a single relation scheme instead of three. Let us consider the following scheme.

$$\begin{aligned} database(\quad & employee\_name : VARCHAR(24), \\ & address : VARCHAR(36), \\ & department\_name : VARCHAR(24), \\ & manager\_name : VARCHAR(24), \\ & manager\_address : VARCHAR(36), \\ & location : VARCHAR(36), \\ & budget : NUMERIC, \\ & date : DATE) \end{aligned}$$

In Chapters 7 and 8, we study tools and techniques for the design of a database application, namely the Entity-Relationship diagrams and the decomposition into normal forms, respectively. These tools and techniques help us to design a 'good' schema or to choose among alternative designs. As an exercise, the reader is invited to think about possible schemas for the example, and about their respective advantages and disadvantages.

If we forbid null values, we realise that the choice of a particular schema imposes constraints on the data. It is not possible to record an employee without an address following the schema of the previous section. In the schema above with a single relation it is not possible to record an employee without assigning her to a department. It seems indeed that these choices depend on the logic of the application: Can an employee be hired and not assigned to a department? Can an employee work for more than one department? Can an employee not have an address (or can her address be unknown)? The answers to these questions define business rules that the designer of the database application tries and translates into appropriate relation schemes, in which they are implicitly enforced by structural constraints, as well as into explicit integrity constraints.

Definition 2.6 *An integrity constraint is a rule that must be verified by every instance of a relational database schema.*

States of the database must be valid or consistent with respect to the integrity constraints. Transactions that bring the database into states violating the integrity constraints are not acceptable.

Without going into the formal and detailed definitions, we introduce the main categories of integrity constraints: functional dependencies, multi-valued dependencies, inclusion dependencies, unique constraints, not null constraints and generalised dependencies. These correspond to the categories of constraints that can be expressed in SQL (see Chapter 5).

Functional dependencies indicate that the value of certain attributes is determined by the value of other attributes. Typically, knowing the social security number of a person determines her name, address and other personal information since it identifies the person. We study functional dependencies extensively in Chapter 8 since they play a crucial rule in designing 'good' schemas. If a set of attributes in the scheme of a relation determines the entire scheme, this set of attributes is called a *key*. There may be several keys for a given relation scheme. The designer chooses a primary key (refer to the discussion in Chapter 8 about the difference between a primary key as declared in SQL and the theoretical definition of a primary key). The primary key may be represented in the scheme by underlining the participating attributes. For instance, we indicate that the name of an employee and the name of a department form a primary key for the relation `work_for` as follows.

$$work\_for(\quad \underline{employee\_name}: VARCHAR(24),$$
$$\underline{department\_name}: VARCHAR(24),$$
$$date: DATE)$$

Since values of attributes in the relational model in first normal form are atomic, sets of values must be represented by several t-uples. For example, in an instance of the *work_for* relation from the relational database schema given above, each department for which a given employee works would be represented by a different t-uple. When several independent such sets are combined in the same relation – for example, an employee, the department she works for and the skills she possesses – one must make sure that the elements of the several sets are combined properly. Each possible combination of department and skill of an employee must be available in one t-uple of the relation instance for this employee. Such rules are expressed by means of multi-valued dependencies.

Inclusion dependencies indicate that the value of certain attributes in one relation must also be the value of other attributes in a possibly different relation. The referential integrity constraint (also called foreign key constraint) is a typical example of inclusion dependency. In this case, the values of some attributes in one relation must be the values of primary key attributes in another relation. For example, in an instance of the *work_for* relation, a value of the attribute *employee_name* must be a value of the attribute *employee_name* in the instance of the *employee* relation. Similarly, in an instance of the *work_for* relation presented above, a value of the attribute *department_name* must be a value of the attribute *department_name* in the instance of the *department* relation. In other words, we must make sure that we are referencing inside the `work_for` relation existing employees and departments.

Unique constraints indicate that the combination of values for certain attributes can appear in one t-uple at most in the entire relation instance.

Not null constraints indicate that the null value is not an acceptable value for certain attributes.

Finally, generalised dependencies are any other constraint that can be expressed as a condition on the state of the database with the query language at hand: algebra, calculus or SQL.

Chapter 3

Relational Calculus

3.1 Logic and Calculus

We have now a logical data model, the relational model to represent and store data. In order to query data, we need query languages. In this chapter, we define successively two query languages based on t-uple relational calculus and domain relational calculus, respectively. Since both calculi are based on first order logic, we first recall some basic concepts.

Both domain and t-uple relational calculi define the syntax and semantics of formulae. The formulae of both calculi are logical formulae of first order logic. They are used to express queries. The variables of domain calculus formulae range over individual values in the domains of the attributes of the relations. The variables of t-uple calculus formulae range over t-uples. Informally, the result of a query expressed with a formula is the set of values that can be assigned to some (free) variables in the formula in order to make the formula true. This is very similar to the notation one uses to define sets in intention (as opposed to in extension). For example, the set $S = \{1, 2, 3\}$ is hereby defined in extension. A definition in intention of the same set is: $S = \{X \mid X \in \mathbb{N} \land 0 < X < 4\}$, where X is a variable and $\mathbb{N}$ the set of integers. The set contains the values that can be substituted for X to make the expression (or formula) $1 < X < 4$ true. Although the two calculi have different meanings and ranges for their variables, they are very similar. Their semantics relies on first order logic, which in turn is an extension of propositional logic.

We recall here the semantics of the main logical connectives of propositional and first order logic by giving their truth tables. Let us assume that P and Q are propositions that can be true or false. The truth table of the formula $P \land Q$, which denotes the *conjunction*, or 'and', of P and Q, is given in Figure 3.1. The truth table of the formula $P \lor Q$, which denotes the *disjunction*, or 'or', of P and Q, is shown in Figure 3.2. Figure 3.3 illustrates the truth table of the formula $\neg Q$, which denotes the *negation* of Q. The truth table of the formula $P \Rightarrow Q$, which denotes the *implication* of Q by P, is given in Figure 3.4. Connectives can be expressed one in terms of another. For instance, implication can be expressed in terms of negation and disjunction or conjunction ($\equiv$ denotes equivalent formulae, i.e., formulae that have the same truth table): $(P \Rightarrow Q) \equiv (\neg P \vee Q) \equiv \neg(P \wedge \neg Q)$.

First order logic differs from propositional logic in that it also allows variables and quantifiers. We present the corresponding syntax and semantics for both calculi in the sections that follow.

3.2 T-uple Relational Calculus (TRC)

3.2.1 The Syntax of TRC

In this section, we are only interested in defining the well-formed formulae of t-uple relational calculus or TRC. This section does not deal with the meaning, or semantics, of the calculus. Its sole purpose is to give the rules according to which a formula can be declared syntactically correct or not.

Formulae in the t-uple relational calculus are constructed from the following sets:

- A set $\mathcal{D}$ of values (constants), which is the union of all the domains of the attributes of the relations involved. By convention, values are quoted, are a number or start with a lowercase.

- A set $\mathcal{X}$ of variables. By convention, variables start with an uppercase.

- A set $\mathcal{R}$ of relation names. In this chapter, all relation names start with a lowercase to distinguish them from variables.

- A set $\mathcal{A}$ of attribute names. In this chapter, all attribute names start with a lowercase to distinguish them from variables.

- A set $\mathcal{B}$ of operators such as $=, <, > \leq, \geq$ etc., as appropriate to the various domains involved.

- The set $\{\forall, \exists, \wedge, \vee, \neg, \Rightarrow\}$ of quantifiers and connectives.

Section 3.2. T-uple Relational Calculus (TRC)

P	Q	$P \wedge Q$
true	true	true
true	false	false
false	true	false
false	false	false

Figure 3.1: Truth Table of Conjunction

P	Q	$P \vee Q$
true	true	true
true	false	true
false	true	true
false	false	false

Figure 3.2: Truth Table of Disjunction

Q	$\neg Q$
true	false
false	true

Figure 3.3: Truth Table of Negation

P	Q	$P \Rightarrow Q$
true	true	true
true	false	false
false	true	true
false	false	true

Figure 3.4: Truth Table of Implication

The calculus also uses the three symbols (,) and .. The symbols $\forall$ and $\exists$ represent the universal and existential quantifiers, respectively. In English they are read 'for all' and 'there exist', respectively. We call *terms* both values and expressions of the form $X.a$ where X is a variable and a is an attribute name. This section only differs from the one about domain relational calculus in matters concerning the terms and their interpretation.

Definition 3.1 *A well-formed atomic formula of t-uple relational calculus is an expression of the form:*

- T_1 *op* T_2, *where* T_1 *and* T_2 *are terms, and op an operator in* $\mathcal{B}$;
- $X \in r$, *where X is a variable and r a relation in* $\mathcal{R}$.

From atomic formulae we can recursively build complex formulae.

Definition 3.2 *A well-formed formula is an expression of the form:*

- F, *where F is a well-formed atomic formula;*
- *an expression with connectives:*
    - $(F_1 \wedge F_2)$, *where F_1 and F_2 are well-formed formulae;*
    - $(F_1 \vee F_2)$, *where F_1 and F_2 are well-formed formulae;*
    - $(F_1 \Rightarrow F_2)$, *where F_1 and F_2 are well-formed formulae;*
    - $\neg F$, *where F is a well-formed formula;*
- *an expression with quantifiers:*
    - $\forall X F$, *where X is a variable in $\mathcal{V}$ and F is a well-formed formula; we say that $\forall$ governs X;*
    - $\exists X F$, *where X is a variable in $\mathcal{V}$ and F is a well-formed formula; we say that $\exists$ governs X;*
- *we accept flexible use of the parenthesis whenever it is not ambiguous.*

No other expression is a well-formed formula.

Strictly speaking, an expression of the form $(X.a = 11 \wedge (\forall X X \in r))$ is a well-formed formula. However, such a formula is, if not ambiguous, confusing. Indeed, the variable X outside the scope of the quantifier and the variable X inside the scope of the universal quantifier are actually different variables from the point of view of semantics. This lack of readability can easily be overcome by renaming one of the variables $Y.a = 11 \wedge (\forall X X \in R)$. Therefore, as a convention, we require that different variables be given different names. This implies that a variable is either not governed by a quantifier or solely governed by one quantifier. In other words, if there exists a sub-expression of the form $(\forall X F)$ or $(\exists X F)$, then X should not appear outside F. For the sake of simplicity, we give the following definition under this assumption.

Definition 3.3 *Given F a well-formed formula of t-uple relational calculus, a variable X in F is a free variable if and only if it is not governed by a quantifier in F.*

3.2.2 The Semantics of TRC

Given a database instance, an interpretation of a t-uple relational calculus formula is a mapping I of the well-formed formula to the set $\{true, false\}$. I is defined under $\mathcal{D}$, the set of all permissible values in the domains. An interpretation essentially maps every free variable to a t-uple of values in one of the Cartesian products $\mathcal{D}^n$ for some $n \in \mathbb{N}$.

We denote $F[X/t]$ the formula F in which all occurrences of the variable X are replaced by the t-uple t.

Definition 3.4 *A mapping I from the set of well-formed formulae to the set $\{true, false\}$ is an interpretation of a t-uple relational calculus formula if and only if it maps the formula in the following ways:*

- *$I(v) = v$, if v is a value in $\mathcal{D}$;*

- *$I(X) = t$, if X is a variable in $\mathcal{X}$ and t is a t-uple of values in one of the Cartesian products $\mathcal{D}^n$ for any n;*

- *$I(X \in r) = true$ if $r(I(X))$ belongs to the database instance and $false$ otherwise, if r is a relation in $\mathcal{R}$ and X is a variable in $\mathcal{X}$;*

- $I(T_1 \text{ op } T_2) = I(T_1) \text{ op } I(T_2))$, where op is an operator in $\mathcal{B}$ and T_1 and T_2 are terms (variables or values);

- $I((F_1 \wedge F_2)) = (I(F_1) \wedge I(F_2))$, where F_1 and F_2 are well-formed formulae;

- $I((F_1 \vee F_2)) = (I(F_1) \vee I(F_2))$, where F_1 and F_2 are well-formed formulae;

- $I((F_1 \Rightarrow F_2)) = (I(F_1) \Rightarrow I(F_2))$, where F_1 and F_2 are well-formed formulae;

- $I(\neg F) = \neg(I(F))$, where F is a well-formed formula;

- $I(\exists X F) = \bigvee_{t \in \mathcal{D}^n} I(F[X/t])$, where F is a well-formed formula, X a variable in $\mathcal{X}$ and $n \in \mathbb{N}$;

- $I(\forall X F) = \bigwedge_{t \in \mathcal{D}^n} I(F[X/t])$, where F is a well-formed formula, X a variable in $\mathcal{X}$ and $n \in \mathbb{N}$.

The above definition is long and may look complicated but it is, in fact, rather simple. It essentially says that connectives, $\vee$, $\wedge$, $\neg$ and $\Rightarrow$, have to be interpreted as in propositional logic. Constants, that we have called values, can be interpreted as themselves.

A universally quantified formula is interpreted as the conjunction of all the possible formulae obtained by removing the quantification and by replacing the quantified variable by a t-uple of values in the original formula. Therefore, the universally quantified formula is true if and only if each one of the formulae in which the variable is replaced by a t-uple of values after the quantification is removed is true, or, simply put, if it is true for all the possible t-uples of values. It is false otherwise.

An existentially quantified formula is interpreted as the disjunction of all the possible formulae obtained by removing the quantification and by replacing the quantified variable by a t-uple of values in the original formula. Therefore, the existentially quantified formula is true if and only if at least one of the formulae in which the variable is replaced by a t-uple of values after the quantification is removed is true, or, simply put, if it is true for some t-uple of values. It is false otherwise.

The truth value of the interpretation of a term of the form $t \in r$ is given by the t-uple t in the instance of r in the database instance. In other words, $t \in r$ is true if and only if the t-uple t is in the relation instance r.

Most importantly, free variables are replaced by t-uples of constants or values. Each t-uple defines a different interpretation.

Finally, the reader will remember from Chapter 2 that $t.a$ denotes the value of the attribute a of t-uple t.

Let us, for example, consider the database instance containing an instance of the relation **department** as illustrated in Figure 3.5.

department_name	location	manager	budget
accounting	107 Jurong Road	Paul Smith	1000000
human resource	10 Western Plaza	Jeremy Sentoso	900000
marketing	107 Jurong Road	Emilda Ramakuti	400000
operations	10 Western Plaza	Emy Laurent	1500000
sales	107 Jurong Road	Peter Ho	2000000

Figure 3.5: Instance of the *department* Relation

The following formula is true for all interpretations with respect to the database instance.

$\exists T (T \in department$

$\wedge T.department\_name =' marketing'$

$\wedge T.location =' 107\ Jurong\ Road'$

$\wedge T.manager =' Emilda\ Ramakuti'$

$\wedge T.budget = 400000).$

The following t-uple belongs to the instance of the relation *department* in the database instance and makes the above formula true if substituted for the variable T.

$('marketing',' 107\ Jurong\ Road',' Emilda\ Ramakuti', 400000).$

For the same reason, the following formula is also true (for all interpretations and with respect to the database instance).

$\exists T(T \in department$
$\wedge T.location =' 107\ Jurong\ Road'$
$\wedge T.manager =' Emilda\ Ramakuti'$
$\wedge T.budget < 1000000).$

However, the following formula is false (for all interpretations and with respect to the database instance).

$\forall T(T \in department \Rightarrow ($
$T.location =' 107\ Jurong\ Road'$
$\wedge T.manager =' Emilda\ Ramakuti'$
$\wedge T.budget = 400000)).$

Indeed, not all the t-uples in the instance of the relation *department* are of the following form, where v is some value.

$(v,' 107\ Jurong\ Road','Emilda\ Ramakuti', 400000).$

We are, of course, interested in those interpretations, i.e., in those values of the free variables that make the formula true. Such interpretations are called models.

Definition 3.5 *An interpretation of a formula F is a model of F if and only if it maps F to true: $I(F) = true$.*

3.2.3 Queries in TRC

A query in t-uple relational calculus is a definition in intention of the set of answers to the queries under the semantics we have presented above. A query is a device that collects possible values of the free variables that can make the formula defining the query true under some interpretation.

Section 3.2. T-uple Relational Calculus (TRC)

Definition 3.6 *A query in t-uple relational calculus is of the form:*

$\{t \mid \exists I \; a \; model \; of \; F \; such \; that$
$I(T) = t \; for \; T \; a \; free \; variable \; of \; F\}.$

We concede that the above form, although precise, is impractical and unnecessarily complicated. For this reason, we use the following shorthand.

$\{T \mid F\}.$

It is necessary that the variable in the head of the query be a free variable. It is not necessary that all variables not in the head of the query be quantified. Indeed, according to the semantics we give, free variables not present in the head of the query behave similarly to existentially quantified variables. We nevertheless suggest that the reader tries and quantifies all the variables not in the head of the query in order to avoid confusion, even though the resulting expression is longer: the variable in the head is the only free variable. By convention, the attributes of a t-uple variable T in the head of a query are those mentioned explicitly, e.g.,$T.a = \cdots$, or explicitly, e.g. $T \in r$.

We can now try and express simple queries using the example of the database instance presented in Chapter 1. Let us print the names and addresses of all the employees. This can be expressed by the following query.

$\{T \mid T \in employee\}.$

Let us print the names of the employees working for a department and the name of their manager in the department. This can be expressed by the following query.

$\{S \mid \exists T1 \exists T2 \exists T3 ($
$\quad T1 \in employee$
$\quad \wedge T2 \in work\_for$
$\quad \wedge T3 \in department$
$\quad \wedge T1.employee\_name = T2.employee\_name$
$\quad \wedge T2.department\_name = T3.department\_name$
$\quad \wedge S.employee\_name = T1.employee\_name$
$\quad \wedge S.manager = T3.manager)\}.$

Finally, let us print the names of those employees not working for a department. This can be expressed by the following query.

$\{S \mid \exists T1 \forall T2($
$\quad T1 \in employee$
$\quad \wedge (T2 \in work\_for$
$\quad \Rightarrow T1.employee\_name <> T2.employee\_name)$
$\quad \wedge S.employee\_name = T1.employee\_name)\}.$

3.3 Domain Relational Calculus (DRC)

3.3.1 The Syntax of DRC

In this section, we are only interested in defining the well-formed formulae of domain relational calculus or DRC. This section does not deal with the meaning, or semantics, of the calculus. Its sole purpose is to give the rules according to which a formula can be declared syntactically correct or not.

Formulae in the domain relational calculus are constructed from the following sets:

- A set $\mathcal{D}$ of values (constants), which is the union of all the domains of the attributes of the relations involved. By convention, values are quoted, are numbers or start with a lowercase.

- A set $\mathcal{X}$ of variables. By convention, variables start with a uppercase.

- A set $\mathcal{R}$ of relation names. In this chapter all relation names start with a lowercase to distinguish them from variables.

- A set $\mathcal{B}$ of operators such as $=, <, > \leq, \geq$ etc., as appropriate to the various domains involved.

- The set $\{\forall, \exists, \wedge, \vee, \neg, \Rightarrow\}$ of quantifiers and connectives.

The calculus also uses the two symbols (and). We call terms values and variables. This section only differs from the one about t-uple relational calculus in matters concerning the terms and their interpretation.

Section 3.3. Domain Relational Calculus (DRC)   29

Definition 3.7 *A well-formed atomic formula of domain relational calculus is an expression of the form:*

- T_1 *op* T_2, *where* T_1 *and* T_2 *are terms in* $\mathcal{D} \cup \mathcal{X}$, *and op an operator in* $\mathcal{B}$;

- $r(T_1, ..., T_n)$, *where* T_1 *to* T_n *are terms in* $\mathcal{D} \cup \mathcal{X}$, *and r a relation in* $\mathcal{R}$ *with n attributes in its scheme;*

From atomic formulae we can recursively build complex formulae.

Definition 3.8 *A well-formed formula is an expression of the form:*

- *F, where F is a well-formed atomic formula;*

- *an expression with connectives:*

    - $(F_1 \wedge F_2)$, *where* F_1 *and* F_2 *are well-formed formulae;*
    - $(F_1 \vee F_2)$, *where* F_1 *and* F_2 *are well-formed formulae;*
    - $(F_1 \Rightarrow F_2)$, *where* F_1 *and* F_2 *are well-formed formulae;*
    - $\neg F$, *where F is a well-formed formula;*

- *an expression with quantifiers:*

    - $\forall X F$, *where X is a variable in* $\mathcal{V}$ *and F is a well-formed formula; we say that $\forall$ governs X;*
    - $\exists X F$, *where X is a variable in* $\mathcal{V}$ *and F is a well-formed formula; we say that $\exists$ governs X;*

- *we accept flexible use of the parenthesis whenever it is not ambiguous.*

No other expression is a well-formed formula.

Strictly speaking, an expression of the form $(X = 11 \wedge (\forall X r(X)))$ is a well-formed formula. However, such a formula is, if not ambiguous, confusing. Indeed, the variable X outside the scope of the quantifier and the variable X inside the scope of the quantifier are actually different variables from the point of view of semantics. This lack of readability can easily be overcome by renaming one of the variables: $Y = 11 \land (\forall X r(X))$. Therefore, as a convention, we require that different variables be given different names. This implies that a variable is either not governed by a quantifier or solely governed by one quantifier. In other words, if there exists a sub-expression of the form $(\forall X F)$ or $(\exists X F)$, then X should not appear outside F. For the sake of simplicity, we give the following definition under this assumption.

Definition 3.9 *Given F a well-formed formula of domain relational calculus, a variable X in F is a free variable if and only if it is not governed by a quantifier in F.*

3.3.2 The Semantics of DRC

Given a database instance, an interpretation of a domain relational calculus formula is a mapping I of the well-formed formula to the set $\{true, false\}$. I is defined under $\mathcal{D}$, the set of all permissible values in the domains. An interpretation essentially maps every free variable to a value in $\mathcal{D}$.

We denote $F[X/v]$ the formula F in which all occurrences of the variable X are replaced by the value v.

Definition 3.10 *A mapping I from the set of well-formed formulae to the set $\{true, false\}$ is an interpretation of a domain relational calculus formula if and only if it maps the formula in the following ways:*

- $I(v) = v$, if v is a value in $\mathcal{D}$;

- $I(X) = v$, if X is a variable in $\mathcal{X}$ and v is a value in $\mathcal{D}$;

- $I(r(T_1, ..., T_n)) = true$ if $r(I(T_1), ..., I(T_n))$ belongs to the database instance and $false$ otherwise, if r is a relation in $\mathcal{R}$ and T_1 to T_n are terms (variables or values);

- $I(T_1 \; op \; T_2) = I_t(T_1) \; op \; I_t(T_2))$, where op is an operator in $\mathcal{B}$ and T_1 and T_2 are terms (variables or values);

- $I((F_1 \land F_2)) = (I(F_1) \land I(F_2))$, where F_1 and F_2 are well-formed formulae;

- $I((F_1 \vee F_2)) = (I(F_1) \vee I(F_2))$, where F_1 and F_2 are well-formed formulae;

- $I((F_1 \Rightarrow F_2)) = (I(F_1) \Rightarrow I(F_2))$, where F_1 and F_2 are well-formed formulae;

- $I(\neg F) = \neg(I(F))$, where F is a well-formed formula;

- $I(\exists X F) = \bigvee_{v \in \mathcal{D}} I(F[X/v])$, where F is a well-formed formula and X a variable in $\mathcal{X}$;

- $I(\forall X F) = \bigwedge_{v \in \mathcal{D}} I(F[X/v])$, where F is a well-formed formula and X a variable in $\mathcal{X}$.

The above definition is long and may look complicated but it is, in fact, rather simple. It essentially says that connectives, $\vee$, $\wedge$, $\neg$ and $\Rightarrow$, have to be interpreted as in propositional logic. Constants or values can be interpreted as themselves.

A universally quantified formula is interpreted as the conjunction of all the possible formulae obtained by removing the quantification and by replacing the quantified variable by a value in the original formula. Therefore, the universally quantified formula is true if and only if each one of the formulae in which the variable is replaced by a value after the quantification is removed is true, or, simply put, if it is true for all the possible values. It is false otherwise.

An existentially quantified formula is interpreted as the disjunction of all the possible formulae obtained by removing the quantification and by replacing the quantified variable by a value in the original formula. Therefore, the existentially quantified formula is true if and only if at least one of the formulae in which the variable is replaced by a value after the quantification is removed is true, or, simply put, if it is true for some value. It is false otherwise.

The truth value of the interpretation of a ground term (i.e., a term not containing variables) of the form $r(v_n, ..., v_n)$ is given by the t-uple $(v_1, ..., v_n)$ in the instance of r in the database instance. In other words, $r(v_n, ..., v_n)$ is true if and only if the t-uple $(v_n, ..., v_n)$ is in the relation instance r.

Most importantly, free variables are replaced by constants or values. Each constant defines a different interpretation.

Let us, for example, consider the database instance containing an instance of the relation **department** as illustrated in Figure 3.5. The following formula is true for all interpretations with respect to the database instance.

$department('marketing', '107\ Jurong\ Road', 'Emilda\ Ramakuti', 400000).$

The following t-uple belongs to the instance of the relation *department* in the database instance.

$('marketing', '107\ Jurong\ Road', 'Emilda\ Ramakuti', 400000).$

For the same reason, an interpretation mapping Y to 400000 also maps the following formula to true.

$\exists X (department(X, '107\ Jurong\ Road', 'Emilda\ Ramakuti', Y)$
$\wedge Y < 1000000).$

However, the following formula is false (for all interpretations and with respect to the database instance).

$\forall X \forall Y \forall Z \forall T (department(X, Y, Z, T) \Rightarrow ($
$Y =' 107\ Jurong\ Road' \wedge Z =' Emilda\ Ramakuti' \wedge T = 400000)).$

Indeed, not all the t-uples in the instance of the relation *department* are of the following form, where v is some value.

$(v, '107\ Jurong\ Road', 'Emilda\ Ramakuti', 400000).$

We are, of course, interested in those interpretations, i.e., those sets of values of the free variables that make the formula true. Such interpretations are called models.

Definition 3.11 *An interpretation of a formula F is a model of F if and only if it maps F to true: $I(F) = true$.*

3.3.3 Queries in DRC

A query in domain relational calculus is a definition in intention of the set of answers to the queries under the semantics we have presented above. A query is a device that collects possible values of the free variables that can make the formula defining the query true under some interpretation.

Definition 3.12 *A query in domain relational calculus is of the form:*

$\{< v_1, \cdots, v_n >| \exists I$ *a model of* F *such that*
$I(X_1) = v_1, \cdots, I(X_n) = v_n$ *for* $X_1, \cdots, X_n$ *free variables of* $F\}$.

We concede that the above form, although precise, is impractical and unnecessarily complicated. For this reason, we use the following shorthand.

$\{< X_1, \cdots, X_n >| F\}$.

It is necessary that variables in the head of the query be free variables. It is not necessary that all variables not in the head of the query be quantified. Indeed, according to the semantics we give, free variables not present in the head of the query behave similarly to existentially quantified variables. We nevertheless suggest that the reader tries and quantifies all the variables not in the head of the query in order to avoid confusion: the variables in the head are the only free variables.

We can now try and express simple queries using the example of the database instance presented in Chapter 1. Let us print the names and addresses of all the employees. This can be expressed by the following query.

$\{< N, A >| employee(N, A)\}$.

Let us now print the names of the employees working for a department and the name of their manager in the department. This can be expressed by the following query.

$\{< E, M >| \exists A \exists D \exists Da \exists L \exists B$
$(employee(E, A)$
$\wedge work\_for(E, D, Da)$
$\wedge department(D, L, M, B))\}$.

Finally, let us print the names of those employees not working for a department. This can be expressed by the following query.

$$\{<E>|\ \exists A \forall D \forall Da (employee(E,A) \land \neg work\_for(E,D,Da))\}.$$

3.4 Safety

Let us consider the relation *department* as illustrated in Figure 3.5. Let us examine the following query in domain relational calculus.

$$\{<D>|\ \exists M \exists B \neg department(D,'107\ Jurong\ Road', M, B)\}.$$

It may seem, at first glance, that the above query denotes the names of the departments not located at 107 Jurong Road. This is, however, not the case. Let us look at the interpretations and models of the formula defining the query:

$$I(\exists M \exists B \neg department(DN,'107\ Jurong\ Road', M, B)).$$

We can rewrite this expression as follows according to the definition of an interpretation:

$$\bigvee_{v_1 \in \mathcal{D}} (\bigvee_{v_2 \in \mathcal{D}} \neg department(v_0,'107\ Jurong\ Road', v_1, v_2)).$$

From the above, we see that an interpretation is a model of the formula if and only if there exist some values v_0, v_1 and v_2 such that the following t-uple does not belong to the instance of the relation *department*.

$$(v_0,'107\ Jurong\ Road', v_1, v_2).$$

For any value $v_0 \in \mathcal{D}$ it is possible to find values v_1 and v_2 such that $(v_0,'107\ Jurong\ Road', v_1, v_2)$ is not a t-uple in *department*. Therefore, the result of the query is $\mathcal{D}$, which is possibly infinite as it may contain the set of integers, for instance.

Queries in both t-uple relational calculus and domain relational calculus may display this pathology. Such queries should be avoided since they potentially yield impractical infinite results. It is possible in both t-uple and domain calculus to define a class of queries which will not suffer from this problem. Queries in the class are called *safe*. Informally, queries are safe if each variable can be mapped to a value (in DRC) or a t-uple of values (TRC) that is contained in or related to an instance of a relation. For instance, the query that denotes the names of the departments not located at 107 Jurong Road, can be written as follows.

$$\{< D >|\ \exists L \exists M \exists B (department(D, L, M, B) \wedge L \neq' 107\ Jurong\ Road')\}.$$

It is safe because every variable appears in a positive (non-negated) occurrence of *department*.

Unsafe queries are therefore often the result of errors in the usage of negation, universal quantification and disjunction (and also implication since it is a combination of negation and disjunction, and possibly hides universal quantification). Care should be exercised when writing queries with such quantifiers and connectives.

Chapter 4
Relational Algebra

4.1 Operators and Composability

Relational algebra is a query language. Although, as we will see, it has an imperative flavour ("do this in order to compute the result of the query") it must be remembered that it is not an imperative language. Indeed, a query in relational algebra is an expression that denotes a set of t-uples (the answer to the query) independently of any particular system, implementation and evaluation mechanism. We should rather say that relational algebra is operational. Indeed, it uses operators and combinations of operators as opposed to relational calculus (see Chapter 3) and SQL (see Chapter 5) that use logical formulae. In this chapter, we give the definitions of the main relational algebra operators in terms of t-uple relational calculus.

Relation instances are sets. Database instances are sets of relation instances. It seems reasonable to consider queries whose results are relation instances. Indeed if simple queries return relation instances, they can be used inside new queries to build complex expressions and recursively. This property is called composability. Relational algebra operators operate on one or more relation instances and denote a relation instance. Relational algebra queries can be composed together to form arbitrarily complex queries.

4.2 Standard Set Operators

Since relation instances are sets, the first operators of relational algebra that we present are the standard set operators: *union*, *intersection* and *non-symmetric difference*. To illustrate these operators we use the relation instances *employee*1 and *employee*2 shown in Figures 4.1 and 4.2, respectively. In this section we omit the square brackets around the relation name to refer to its instance and we use the terms 'relation instances' and 'relations', indistinctly.

employee_name	address
Jain Singh	10 Johor Way
John McMallen	107 Jln Kampung Baru
Kwok Li Shin	19 Johor Way
Nancy Santi	123 Pantai Street
Paul Smith	22 Bukit Ridge
Peter Ho	22 Bukit Ridge
Putri Bte Mohamed	12 Raffles Road
Reza Ernawati	19 Johor Way
Wang Chee Leong	100 Centre Point
Yao Chen	123 Pantai Street

figure 4.1: Instance of the *employee*1 Relation

employee_name	address
Emilda Ramakuti	101 East Coast Crescent
Emy Laurent	107 Jurong Road
Jeremy Sentoso	107 Jurong Road
John McMallen	107 Jln Kampung Baru
Kwok Li Shin	19 Johor Way
Nancy Santi	123 Pantai Street
Peter Ho	22 Bukit Ridge
Putri Bte Mohamed	12 Raffles Road
Reza Ernawati	19 Johor Way
Zhou Li	19 Bencoolen Lane

Figure 4.2: Instance of the *employee*2 Relation

Definition 4.1 *The union of two relation instances R1 and R2 is noted and defined as:*

$$R_1 \cup R_2 = \{T \mid T \in R1 \vee T \in R2\}.$$

Section 4.2. Standard Set Operators   39

Figure 4.3 shows the result of the evaluation of the union:

$employee1 \cup employee2$.

Notice that elements in both sets *employee1* and *employee2* appear only once in the result since it is a set.

employee_name	address
Emilda Ramakuti	101 East Coast Crescent
Emy Laurent	107 Jurong Road
Jain Singh	10 Johor Way
Jeremy Sentoso	107 Jurong Road
John McMallen	107 Jln Kampung Baru
Kwok Li Shin	19 Johor Way
Nancy Santi	123 Pantai Street
Paul Smith	22 Bukit Ridge
Peter Ho	22 Bukit Ridge
Putri Bte Mohamed	12 Raffles Road
Reza Ernawati	19 Johor Way
Wang Chee Leong	100 Centre Point
Yao Chen	123 Pantai Street
Zhou Li	19 Bencoolen Lane

Figure 4.3: Union

Definition 4.2 *The intersection of two relation instances R1 and R2 is noted and defined as:*

$R_1 \cap R_2 = \{T \mid T \in R1 \land T \in R_2\}$.

Figure 4.4 shows the result of the evaluation of the intersection:

$employee1 \cap employee2$.

employee_name	address
John McMallen	107 Jln Kampung Baru
Kwok Li Shin	19 Johor Way
Nancy Santi	123 Pantai Street
Peter Ho	22 Bukit Ridge
Putri Bte Mohamed	12 Raffles Road
Reza Ernawati	19 Johor Way

Figure 4.4: Intersection

Definition 4.3 *The non-symmetric difference, or difference, between two relation instances R1 and R2 is noted and defined as:*

$R_1 - R_2 = \{T \mid T \in R1 \wedge T \notin R2\}.$

Figure 4.5 shows the result of the evaluation of the non-symmetric difference:

$employee2 - employee1.$

employee_name	address
Emilda Ramakuti	101 East Coast Crescent
Emy Laurent	107 Jurong Road
Jeremy Sentoso	107 Jurong Road
Zhou Li	19 Bencoolen Lane

Figure 4.5: Difference

For these three operators, in order to obtain results that are homogeneous sets (relation instances), we need both inputs to be instances of relations with compatible schemes. The relation names may be different, but the attribute names and domains must be identical in both relations. Such relations are said to be *union-compatible*.

At this point, notice that intersection can be expressed in terms of difference. Indeed, for two relation instances R and S, $R \cap S = ((R \cup S) - (R - S)) - (S - R)$. This remark poses the question of minimal sets of operators for relational algebra, which we do not discuss in this book and leave as food for thought for the reader.

4.3 Operators Involving the Structure of Relations

Since relation instances contain structured elements, we can define operators that utilise their structure.

Selection is an operator that selects t-uples of a relation that verify a given condition. The condition, called θ-condition, can be any Boolean expression involving the comparison of attribute values and constants.

Definition 4.4 *Let C be a formula of t-uple relational calculus constructed over the set of attribute names belonging to R and containing a single variable, namely X, such that X is a free variable of C. The selection of a relation instance R according to C is noted and defined as:*

$$\sigma_C(R) = \{T \mid T \in R \wedge C[X/T]\}.$$

In practice, X is written R in the expression of the condition C to denote that X is a t-uple in R.

Let us consider the relation instances *department* given in Figure 2.1, *work_for* given in Figure 2.2 and *employee* given in Figure 2.3. Figure 4.6 illustrates the result of the evaluation of the selection of all the t-uples such that the budget is below $1000000 from the relation instance department:

$$\sigma_{department.budget<1000000}(department).$$

department_name	location	manager	budget
human resource	10 Western Plaza	Jeremy Sentoso	900000
marketing	107 Jurong Road	Emilda Ramakuti	400000

Figure 4.6: Selection

One can omit the name of the relation in the θ-condition, when it is not ambiguous:

$$\sigma_{budget<1000000}(department).$$

We may also be interested in keeping certain attributes. The *projection* of a relation according to a projection list that is a subset of the relation scheme (i.e., a list of attribute names) denotes the set of sub-t-uples with the given attributes.

Definition 4.5 *Let R be a relation instance. Let L be a subset of the scheme of R. The projection of R according to the projection set L is noted and defined as:*

$$\pi_L(R) = \{T \mid \exists T_1 (T_1 \in R \wedge (\bigwedge_{a \in L} T_1.a = T.a))\}.$$

Figure 4.7 illustrates the result of the evaluation of the projection of the relation instance *department* on the list of attributes (*manager, location*):

$$\pi_{\{manager,location\}}(department).$$

manager	location
Paul Smith	107 Jurong Road
Jeremy Sentoso	10 Western Plaza
Emilda Ramakuti	107 Jurong Road
Emy Laurent	10 Western Plaza
Peter Ho	107 Jurong Road

Figure 4.7: Projection

In practice, the projection set can be a projection list. It is noted between parentheses and may contain occurrences of the same attribute (although in such a case the scheme of the result is difficult to define formally):

$$\pi_{(manager,location,location)}(department).$$

Section 4.3. Operators Involving the Structure of Relations   43

Finally, the *Cartesian product* of two relations denotes a third relation combining every t-uple of one relation with every t-uple of the other.

Definition 4.6 *The Cartesian product of two relation instances R_1 and R_2 with the schemes S_1 and S_2 is noted and defined as:*

$$R_1 \times R_2 = \{T \mid \exists T_1 \exists T_2 (T_1 \in R_1 \wedge T_2 \in R_2 \wedge$$
$$(\bigwedge_{a \in S_1} T_1.a = T.a) \wedge$$
$$(\bigwedge_{a \in S_2} T_2.a = T.a))\}.$$

Figure 4.8 illustrates the result of the evaluation of the Cartesian product of the relation instance *department* with the relation instance *work_for*:

$department \times work\_for.$

The cardinality of the result is 70 (5 × 14). The degree of the result is 7. Notice that the result has two attributes named *employee_name*. We differentiate them by prefixing their name with the name of the relation from which they come.

The Cartesian product may not seem very interesting an operator. Yet, combined with selection, it defines the *join*. Join is an operator that allows the controlled combination of relations to express complex queries.

Definition 4.7 *The join of two relation instances R_1 and R_2 according to a condition C is noted and defined as:*

$$R_1 \bowtie_C R_2 = \sigma_C(R_1 \times R_2).$$

Figure 4.9 shows the result of the evaluation of the join of the relation instance *department* with the relation instance *work_for* on the condition that the value of the attribute *department_name* in a t-uple of *department* equals the value of the attribute *department_name* in a t-uple of *work_for*:

$department \bowtie_{department.department\_name=work\_for.department\_name} employee.$

The cardinality of the result is 14. The degree of the result is 7.

department.department_name	location	manager	budget	employee_name	work_for department_name	date
accounting	107 Jurong Road	Paul Smith	1000000	Emy Laurent	operations	12/02/2001
sales	107 Jurong Road	Peter Ho	2000000	Emy Laurent	operations	12/02/2001
human resource	10 Western Plaza	Jeremy Sentoso	900000	Emy Laurent	operations	12/02/2001
operations	10 Western Plaza	Emy Laurent	1500000	Emy Laurent	operations	12/02/2001
marketing	107 Jurong Road	Emilda Ramakuti	400000	Emy Laurent	operations	12/02/2001
accounting	107 Jurong Road	Paul Smith	1000000	Putri Bte Mohamed	accounting	04/03/2002
sales	107 Jurong Road	Peter Ho	2000000	Putri Bte Mohamed	accounting	04/03/2002
human resource	10 Western Plaza	Jeremy Sentoso	900000	Putri Bte Mohamed	accounting	04/03/2002
operations	10 Western Plaza	Emy Laurent	1500000	Putri Bte Mohamed	accounting	04/03/2002
marketing	107 Jurong Road	Emilda Ramakuti	400000	Putri Bte Mohamed	accounting	04/03/2002
accounting	107 Jurong Road	Paul Smith	1000000	Jeremy Sentoso	human resource	04/03/2001
sales	107 Jurong Road	Peter Ho	2000000	Jeremy Sentoso	human resource	04/03/2001
human resource	10 Western Plaza	Jeremy Sentoso	900000	Jeremy Sentoso	human resource	04/03/2001
operations	10 Western Plaza	Emy Laurent	1500000	Jeremy Sentoso	human resource	04/03/2001
marketing	107 Jurong Road	Emilda Ramakuti	400000	Jeremy Sentoso	human resource	04/03/2001
accounting	107 Jurong Road	Paul Smith	1000000	John McMallen	sales	06/12/2001
sales	107 Jurong Road	Peter Ho	2000000	John McMallen	sales	06/12/2001
human resource	10 Western Plaza	Jeremy Sentoso	900000	John McMallen	sales	06/12/2001
operations	10 Western Plaza	Emy Laurent	1500000	John McMallen	sales	06/12/2001
marketing	107 Jurong Road	Emilda Ramakuti	400000	John McMallen	sales	06/12/2001
accounting	107 Jurong Road	Paul Smith	1000000	Kwok Li Shin	sales	11/12/2001
sales	107 Jurong Road	Peter Ho	2000000	Kwok Li Shin	sales	11/12/2001
human resource	10 Western Plaza	Jeremy Sentoso	900000	Kwok Li Shin	sales	11/12/2001
operations	10 Western Plaza	Emy Laurent	1500000	Kwok Li Shin	sales	11/12/2001
marketing	107 Jurong Road	Emilda Ramakuti	400000	Kwok Li Shin	sales	11/12/2001
accounting	107 Jurong Road	Paul Smith	1000000	Nancy Santi	human resource	03/03/2001
sales	107 Jurong Road	Peter Ho	2000000	Nancy Santi	human resource	03/03/2001
human resource	10 Western Plaza	Jeremy Sentoso	900000	Nancy Santi	human resource	03/03/2001
operations	10 Western Plaza	Emy Laurent	1500000	Nancy Santi	human resource	03/03/2001
marketing	107 Jurong Road	Emilda Ramakuti	400000	Nancy Santi	human resource	03/03/2001
accounting	107 Jurong Road	Paul Smith	1000000	Paul Smith	accounting	07/05/2001
sales	107 Jurong Road	Peter Ho	2000000	Paul Smith	accounting	07/05/2001
human resource	10 Western Plaza	Jeremy Sentoso	900000	Paul Smith	accounting	07/05/2001
operations	10 Western Plaza	Emy Laurent	1500000	Paul Smith	accounting	07/05/2001
marketing	107 Jurong Road	Emilda Ramakuti	400000	Paul Smith	accounting	07/05/2001
accounting	107 Jurong Road	Paul Smith	1000000	Peter Ho	sales	01/11/2003
sales	107 Jurong Road	Peter Ho	2000000	Peter Ho	sales	01/11/2003
human resource	10 Western Plaza	Jeremy Sentoso	900000	Peter Ho	sales	01/11/2003
operations	10 Western Plaza	Emy Laurent	1500000	Peter Ho	sales	01/11/2003
marketing	107 Jurong Road	Emilda Ramakuti	400000	Peter Ho	sales	01/11/2003
accounting	107 Jurong Road	Paul Smith	1000000	Reza Ernawati	accounting	06/02/2001
sales	107 Jurong Road	Peter Ho	2000000	Reza Ernawati	accounting	06/02/2001
human resource	10 Western Plaza	Jeremy Sentoso	900000	Reza Ernawati	accounting	06/02/2001
operations	10 Western Plaza	Emy Laurent	1500000	Reza Ernawati	accounting	06/02/2001
marketing	107 Jurong Road	Emilda Ramakuti	400000	Reza Ernawati	accounting	06/02/2001
accounting	107 Jurong Road	Paul Smith	1000000	Yao Chen	sales	11/11/2001
sales	107 Jurong Road	Peter Ho	2000000	Yao Chen	sales	11/11/2001
human resource	10 Western Plaza	Jeremy Sentoso	900000	Yao Chen	sales	11/11/2001
operations	10 Western Plaza	Emy Laurent	1500000	Yao Chen	sales	11/11/2001
marketing	107 Jurong Road	Emilda Ramakuti	400000	Yao Chen	sales	11/11/2001
accounting	107 Jurong Road	Paul Smith	1000000	Zhou Li	operations	08/05/2002
sales	107 Jurong Road	Peter Ho	2000000	Zhou Li	operations	08/05/2002
human resource	10 Western Plaza	Jeremy Sentoso	900000	Zhou Li	operations	08/05/2002
operations	10 Western Plaza	Emy Laurent	1500000	Zhou Li	operations	08/05/2002
marketing	107 Jurong Road	Emilda Ramakuti	400000	Zhou Li	operations	08/05/2002
accounting	107 Jurong Road	Paul Smith	1000000	Peter Ho	operations	12/12/2001
sales	107 Jurong Road	Peter Ho	2000000	Peter Ho	operations	12/12/2001
human resource	10 Western Plaza	Jeremy Sentoso	900000	Peter Ho	operations	12/12/2001
operations	10 Western Plaza	Emy Laurent	1500000	Peter Ho	operations	12/12/2001
marketing	107 Jurong Road	Emilda Ramakuti	400000	Peter Ho	operations	12/12/2001
accounting	107 Jurong Road	Paul Smith	1000000	Nancy Santi	sales	01/04/2001
sales	107 Jurong Road	Peter Ho	2000000	Nancy Santi	sales	01/04/2001
human resource	10 Western Plaza	Jeremy Sentoso	900000	Nancy Santi	sales	01/04/2001
operations	10 Western Plaza	Emy Laurent	1500000	Nancy Santi	sales	01/04/2001
marketing	107 Jurong Road	Emilda Ramakuti	400000	Nancy Santi	sales	01/04/2001
accounting	107 Jurong Road	Paul Smith	1000000	Jain Singh	human resource	02/02/2001
sales	107 Jurong Road	Peter Ho	2000000	Jain Singh	human resource	02/02/2001
human resource	10 Western Plaza	Jeremy Sentoso	900000	Jain Singh	human resource	02/02/2001
operations	10 Western Plaza	Emy Laurent	1500000	Jain Singh	human resource	02/02/2001
marketing	107 Jurong Road	Emilda Ramakuti	400000	Jain Singh	human resource	02/02/2001

Figure 4.8: Cartesian Product

Section 4.3. Operators Involving the Structure of Relations

department.department_name	location	manager	budget	employee_name	work_for.department_name	date
operations	10 Western Plaza	Emy Laurent	1500000	Emy Laurent	operations	12/02/2001
accounting	107 Jurong Road	Paul Smith	1000000	Putri Bte Mohamed	accounting	04/03/2002
human resource	10 Western Plaza	Jeremy Sentoso	900000	Jeremy Sentoso	human resource	04/03/2001
sales	107 Jurong Road	Peter Ho	2000000	John McMallen	sales	06/12/2001
sales	107 Jurong Road	Peter Ho	2000000	Kwok Li Shin	sales	11/12/2001
human resource	10 Western Plaza	Jeremy Sentoso	900000	Nancy Santi	human resource	03/03/2001
accounting	107 Jurong Road	Paul Smith	1000000	Paul Smith	accounting	07/05/2001
sales	107 Jurong Road	Peter Ho	2000000	Peter Ho	sales	01/11/2003
accounting	107 Jurong Road	Paul Smith	1000000	Reza Ernawati	accounting	06/02/2001
sales	107 Jurong Road	Peter Ho	2000000	Yao Chen	sales	11/11/2001
operations	10 Western Plaza	Emy Laurent	1500000	Zhou Li	operations	08/05/2002
operations	10 Western Plaza	Emy Laurent	1500000	Peter Ho	operations	12/12/2001
sales	107 Jurong Road	Peter Ho	2000000	Nancy Santi	sales	01/04/2001
human resource	10 Western Plaza	Jeremy Sentoso	900000	Jain Singh	human resource	02/02/2001

Figure 4.9: Join

The combination of a projection with a join on a condition involving a conjunction of equality of attributes is called an *equijoin*. The projection eliminates one of each pair of attributes involved in the equalities since they lead to redundant columns. An equijoin involving all the equalities between attributes with the same name in each relation schemes of the two relations is called a *natural join*. There also exist operators similar to joins that involve the padding of the results with null values. These operators are the *inner-* and *outer-joins*. To distinguish the normal join from these variants, it is sometimes referred to as the θ-join, where θ refers to the θ-condition.

For practical purposes, we also present an operator that is not concerned with the content of the instance but with its scheme. The *renaming* operator creates a copy of a relation instance possibly changing its name and the names of its attributes.

Definition 4.8 *The renaming of a relation instance R of scheme:*

$$R(A_1, A_2, \cdots, A_n)$$

into a relation instance S of scheme:

$$S(B_1, B_2, \cdots, B_n)$$

is noted as:

$$\rho(S, (A_1 \to B_1, A_2 \to B_2, \cdots, A_n \to B_n)(R).$$

An unchanged relation name and unchanged attribute names can be omitted. For readability, we often do not use the renaming operator, instead, for simplicity, use the dot notation to indicate to which relation instance we refer, to avoid ambiguity.

4.4 Queries

We can now try and express queries using combinations of relational operators. Let us, for instance, denote the relation instance containing the names and addresses of the employees who are managers.

$$\pi_{employee.employee\_name, employee.address}($$
$$\sigma_{employee.employee\_name=department.manager}($$
$$employee \times department)).$$

The relation instance denoted is given in Figure 4.10.

employee_name	address
Emilda Ramakuti	101 East Coast Crescent
Emy Laurent	107 Jurong Road
Jeremy Sentoso	107 Jurong Road
Paul Smith	22 Bukit Ridge
Peter Ho	22 Bukit Ridge

Figure 4.10: Managers

The following expression denotes the relation instance containing the names of the employees working for a department and the name of their manager in the department.

$$\pi_{employee.employee\_name, department.manager}($$
$$\sigma_{employee.employee\_name=work\_for.employee_name}$$
$$\wedge work\_for.department\_name=department.department\_name}($$
$$employee \times work\_for \times department)).$$

Section 4.4. Queries

The relation instance denoted is given in Figure 4.11.

employee_name	manager
Emy Laurent	Emy Laurent
Jain Singh	Jeremy Sentoso
Jeremy Sentoso	Jeremy Sentoso
John McMallen	Peter Ho
Kwok Li Shin	Peter Ho
Nancy Santi	Jeremy Sentoso
Nancy Santi	Peter Ho
Paul Smith	Paul Smith
Peter Ho	Emy Laurent
Peter Ho	Peter Ho
Putri Bte Mohamed	Paul Smith
Reza Ernawati	Paul Smith
Yao Chen	Peter Ho
Zhou Li	Emi Laurent

Figure 4.11: Employees and Managers

Finally, the following expression denotes the relation instance containing the names of those employees not working for a department.

$$\pi_{employee.employee\_name}(employee) - \pi_{employee.employee\_name}(work\_for).$$

The relation instance denoted is given in Figure 4.12.

employee_name
Emilda Ramakuti
Wang Chee Leong

Figure 4.12: Employees not Assigned to Any Department

We can compose such expressions to form arbitrarily complex relational algebra queries. Such queries are often best represented in the form of trees. The tree in Figure 4.13 represents the relational algebra expression that denotes the relation instance containing the names of those employees neither working for nor managing a department.

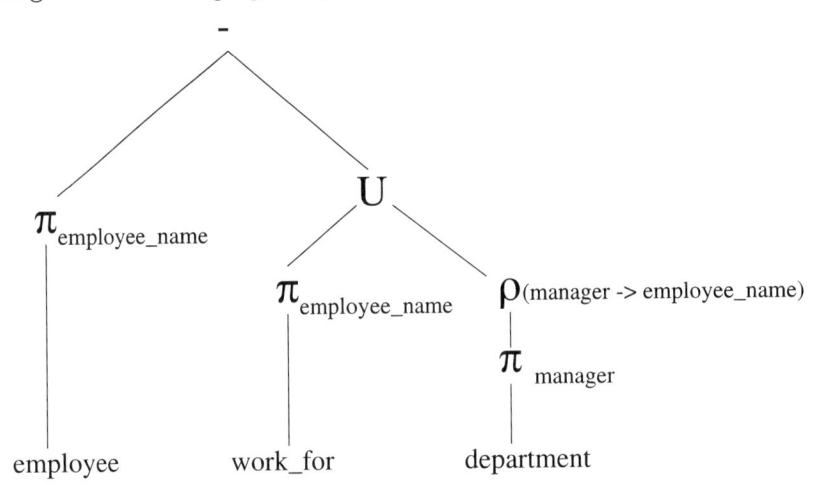

Figure 4.13: A Tree Representation of a Complex Relational Algebra Expression

4.5 The Myth of Declarativeness

We claim and do not prove in this book that both safe calculi and relational algebra are equivalent. This statement means that safe queries expressed in domain relational calculus can be expressed in t-uple relational calculus, that safe queries expressed in t-uple relational calculus can be expressed in relational algebra, and conversely. Yet each language gives a different flavour to the expression of queries. While relational algebra is operational and gives an imperative flavour, domain and t-uple calculi are logical and therefore confer a declarative flavour to the expression of queries. Expressing a query is denoting its result rather than giving indications on how to construct it. The idea of declarativeness contributes to the concepts of physical data independence, logical data independence and knowledge independence. It is a common mistake influenced by the practical study of database system implementation and by database tuning to consider certain queries in algebra or in SQL, for instance, to be inefficient. Certain queries may be inefficiently evaluated by a given algorithm or database management system but queries are never intrinsically inefficient.

Chapter 5
SQL

5.1 A Standard

SQL is an acronym for Structured Query Language. Yet, SQL is not only a query language but also includes statements for several other aspects of the management of database applications. Most SQL statements can be classified into one of the three sets: data definition statements for defining relations, views or constraints; data manipulation statements for updating and querying data and database control statements for defining access rights or concurrency control policies. Thus, as we have seen in Chapter 1, SQL is composed of three sub-languages: the data definition language, or DDL, the data manipulation language, or DML and the database control language, or DCL.

SQL is supported by most commercial database management systems. SQL is an ANSI/ISO/IEC standard. SQL-92 (ANSI X3.135-1992, ISO/IEC 9075:1992) and SQL-99 (ANSI/ISO/IEC 9075: 1999) are the latest two versions of the standard.

Database management systems vendors refer to these standards to define the extent to which their product supports a particular version of SQL. It is rarely the case, if ever, that the complete and exact specification of a given version of the standard is supported.

Furthermore, a single database management system may use different dialects of SQL at different interfaces. It may support a simple interactive SQL for a shell-like user-interface or a comprehensive SQL embedded in a programming language extension, and it may accept dialects from other tools and protocols for interoperability purposes.

In this chapter, we review the main statements of the data definition and data manipulation sub-languages of SQL. The reader is encouraged to check the exact syntax of the SQL dialect of the particular database management system she is using.

5.2 Data Definition Language

Naturally, SQL allows the definition of schemes of relations and the creation of relation instances. The `CREATE TABLE` statement, when executed, results in the creation of an empty relation instance, or table, with the declared relation scheme. In this chapter, we use indifferently the terms 'table', 'relation instance' and 'relation' whenever it is not ambiguous. The following expression is a regular expression defining the general syntax of a simple `CREATE TABLE` statement.

```
CREATE TABLE table_name
  (attribute_name domain
  [, attribute_name domain ]*);
```

The statement is followed by the name of the table, then, by a list, between brackets, of attribute declarations consisting of the name of the attribute followed by its domain. For example, the following statement creates a table named `department` with attributes `department_name`, `location`, `director` and `budget`.

```
CREATE TABLE department
  (department_name VARCHAR(24),
   location VARCHAR(36),
   manager VARCHAR(24),
   budget NUMERIC);
```

The attributes `department_name`, `location` and `manager` in the statement above, are declared to be of type, or domain, string of variable length with maximum length 24 and 36 characters, respectively, and the attribute `budget` is declared to be of type `NUMERIC`. The most common and standard types available in SQL are `CHARACTER(n)` strings of characters, where `n` is the length of the string of characters, `VARCHAR(n)` as seen above, `BIT` Booleans, `NUMERIC`, which covers integers and decimal numbers, `DATE` and `TIME`. Each of these domains comes with functions, operations and operators for comparison that are useful in the expression of queries. The reader is encouraged to check the domains available in the database management system she is using

Section 5.2. Data Definition Language

as well as the functions, operations and comparison operators available for these domains. Some systems also allow the use of user defined types and domains. Such definitions can be expressed by enumeration (if the domain is finite, e.g. days of the week), or by constraining existing domains, as well as, more generally, abstract data types.

The scheme definition and the creation of an empty instance are usually also accompanied by the definition of the column and table level integrity constraints and default values. The following expression is a regular expression defining the complete syntax of a CREATE TABLE statement including the column default values and the column and table constraints.

```
CREATE TABLE table_name
  (attribute_name domain [DEFAULT expr]
  [column_constraint]*
  [,attribute_name domain [DEFAULT expr]
  [column_constraint]* ]*
  [,table_constraint]*);
```

Default values are assigned to some attributes in situations where the values are not given at creation of the t-uple or are deleted as a consequence of a cascading update. For instance, we may decide to assign the default value 'company address' to those employees whose home address is not given, as follows.

```
CREATE TABLE employee
  (employee_name VARCHAR(24) PRIMARY KEY,
  address VARCHAR(36) DEFAULT 'company address');
```

There are five main categories of integrity constraints that can be expressed in SQL: the primary key constraints, the foreign key constraints or referential integrity constraints, the unique constraints, the not null constraints and the generalised dependencies, which can be expressed as any valid condition as allowed in the WHERE clause of an SQL query (see SQL queries below). The syntax of these constraints uses the following keywords: PRIMARY KEY, REFERENCES, UNIQUE, NOT NULL and CHECK, respectively.

The following statement declares a column level constraint that declares the first attribute department_name to be the primary key of the table department. Of course, there can only be one such declaration in a table definition.

```
CREATE TABLE department
  (department_name VARCHAR(24) PRIMARY KEY,
   location VARCHAR(36),
   manager VARCHAR(24),
   budget NUMERIC);
```

If the primary key contains more than one attribute, the constraint must be declared at the table level as follows. In the following example, the set containing the attributes `employee_name` and `department_name` is declared to be the primary key of the table `work_for`.

```
CREATE TABLE work_for
  (employee_name VARCHAR(24),
   department_name VARCHAR(24),
   start_date DATE,
   end_date DATE,
   PRIMARY KEY (employee_name, department_name));
```

Many integrity constraints can be expressed for a single table. In the following example, in addition to the primary key constraint on the attribute `department_name`, three additional constraints are expressed on the attribute `manager`.

```
CREATE TABLE department
  (department_name VARCHAR(24) PRIMARY KEY,
   location VARCHAR(36),
   manager VARCHAR(24) NOT NULL UNIQUE
         REFERENCES employee(employee_name),
   budget NUMERIC);
```

The NOT NULL constraint requires that the system does not accept null values for the attribute. The UNIQUE constraint requires that the values of the attribute be unique in the column of the table. The REFERENCES constraint expresses a foreign key dependency that enforces referential integrity.

Namely, the values of the attribute `manager` must correspond to values of a primary key of the relation `employee`. In other words, the constraints on the attribute `manager` require that every department has a manager which corresponds to an existing employee in the table `employee` and that a manager only manages one department.

Let us now consider a table `task`. The table records the start and end dates and description of the tasks given to the employees in a department for which they work. The definitions of referential integrity constraints and of unique constraints are done at the table level since they involve more than one attribute. The referential integrity constraint requires that a pair of values for the attributes `employee_name` and `department_name` originates from a pair in the table `work_for`, i.e., it requires that the task be given to an existing employee actually working for an existing department. The referenced attributes must constitute a key of the referenced table. The unique constraint requires that a pair of values for the attributes `employee_name` and `start_date` be unique in the table, i.e., it requires that an employee be assigned at most one task for each date. We invite the reader to think about the possible primary keys for this table in the logic of such an application. The following statement declares and creates the table `task`.

```
CREATE TABLE task
  (employee_name VARCHAR(24),
   department_name VARCHAR(24),
   start_date DATE,
   end_date DATE,
   task_description VARCHAR(128),
   FOREIGN KEY(employee_name, department_name)
        REFERENCES work_for(employee_name, department_name),
   UNIQUE(employee_name, start_date));
```

Let us now give examples of column and table level CHECK constraints. CHECK constraints correspond to any Boolean expression in the syntax of the WHERE clauses of SQL queries. The following example shows the expression of a constraint on the attribute `budget` of the `department` table that requires that the value of the budget of any department be strictly above zero.

```
CREATE TABLE department
  (department_name VARCHAR(24) PRIMARY KEY,
   location VARCHAR(36),
   manager VARCHAR(24) NOT NULL UNIQUE
        REFERENCES employee(employee_name),
   budget NUMERIC CHECK (budget > 0));
```

CHECK constraints may be table constraints and involve several attributes. For instance, we may require that the start date of a task be earlier than or equal to its end date.

```
CREATE TABLE task
  (employee_name VARCHAR(24),
   department_name VARCHAR(24),
   start_date DATE,
   end_date DATE,
   task_description VARCHAR(128),
   FOREIGN KEY(employee_name, department_name)
        REFERENCES work_for(employee_name, department_name),
   UNIQUE(employee_name, start_date),
   CHECK (start_date <= end_date));
```

According to the SQL standard it is possible to express a constraint outside the table it concerns by creating an assertion. Assertions are constraints expressed outside the scope of a particular table definition. They may involve more than one table. The reader needs to check whether the database management system that she is using implements assertions.

Assertions are absolutely necessary when the constraint involves several tables. In the following expression, representing the general form of an assertion, assertion_name is a name given to the assertion by the programmer and used by the system when signifying a violation, and constraint is any constraint in the syntax we have seen above.

```
CREATE ASSERTION assertion_name constraint;
```

As an example of a constraint involving the table work_for and table task, we may want to require that for any employee assigned to a task in a

Section 5.2. Data Definition Language

department, the start date of the task be later than or equal to the date at which the employee joined the department. The following assertion checks that there does not exist an employee violating the rule.

```
CREATE ASSERTION task_date
  CHECK(
    NOT EXISTS(
      SELECT work_for.employee_name
      FROM work_for, task
      WHERE work_for.employee_name = task.employee_name
      AND work_for.department_name = task.department_name
      AND work_for.date > task.start_date));
```

Such CHECK constraints may be defined using any expression valid in the WHERE or HAVING clause of an SQL query. It possibly involves complex Boolean expressions, aggregates and nested queries.

Integrity constraints define forbidden situations. By default, integrity constraints are checked immediately after each individual updates. The following statement expresses this default policy explicitly.

```
SET assertion_name IMMEDIATE;
```

Yet, it is possible to request that a particular constraint be checked at the end of a set of updates grouped in a transaction. This is done using the following request.

```
SET constraint_name DEFERRED;
```

Unless advanced constructs not studied here such as triggers are used, a transaction, i.e., a set of updates, violating the constraints is simply rejected by the system. Yet, in the case of referential constraints, SQL allows the programmer to specify simple and natural compensating actions. In the table department as defined above we have required that the manager be a reference to an existing employee. The following statement requests that, if the name of the manager is updated in the table employee, then the corresponding name be updated accordingly in the department table.

```
CREATE TABLE department
  (name VARCHAR(24) PRIMARY KEY,
   location VARCHAR(36),
   manager VARCHAR(24)
          REFERENCES employee(name) ON UPDATE CASCADE,
   budget NUMBER);
```

The following statement requests that if the manager is removed from the table employee the departments that she manages be deleted. If similar compensating actions are requested in the table work_for, the cascade of deletion could propagate to this table and other tables with similar compensating actions, e.g. the table task.

```
CREATE TABLE department
   (name VARCHAR(24) PRIMARY KEY,
    location VARCHAR(36),
    manager VARCHAR(24)
           REFERENCES employee(name) ON DELETE CASCADE,
    budget NUMBER);
```

The default compensating action for every referential constraint is ON DELETE NO ACTION and ON UPDATE NO ACTION. The possible actions are: NO ACTION (default), CASCADE, SET DEFAULT (set the value of foreign key to the indicated default value), SET NULL (set the value of foreign key to the null value).

Instead of creating tables that contain the data that have been explicitly inserted, one can create views. Views are tables whose content is defined by a query. The following expression defines the general syntax of a view definition. The view is given a name and possibly a scheme (attribute names only). The scheme must be compatible with the result of the query. If no scheme is declared, the result of the query implicitly defines the scheme of the view.

```
CREATE VIEW name [(attribute_name [,attribute_name]*)]
AS query;
```

Section 5.2. Data Definition Language

Let us create a view `manager` that contains the names and addresses of the employees who are managers of some departments. Updates to the underlying tables are automatically reflected in the view.

```
CREATE VIEW manager (manager_name, address)
AS SELECT employee.employee_name, employee.address,
          department.department_name
   FROM employee, department
   WHERE employee.employee_name = department.manager;
```

The view can now be queried as if it were a normal table. The following query prints the name, address and department name of every manager.

```
SELECT * FROM manager;
```

Generally, views cannot be updated. There is sometimes no deterministic way to propagate the update to the base relations used in the view definition. Let us, for instance, consider the following view which denotes the average budget of a department.

```
SELECT AVG(budget) FROM department;
```

If we want to increase the average budget there are many ways to update the budget of individual departments. This is called the *view update problem*. SQL, however, authorises updates to views in some cases in which the update is deterministic, for instance, when the view is a selection on a single relation.

Logical data independence and knowledge independence are achieved by means of views. Views also increase the readability of queries. However, in practice, they make the optimisation of queries more complicated for the database management system and may result in less efficient evaluations.

Finally, the definitions of tables, attributes of tables, assertions and views can be dropped or modified as illustrated by the three following statements, deleting the table `task` (with its content), adding an attribute to record the age of an employee (the ages of existing employees would be given a default value if specified or a null value if allowed) and dropping this attribute together with its values for the existing employees, respectively.

```
DROP TABLE task;
```

```
ALTER TABLE employee ADD age NUMERIC;

ALTER TABLE employee DROP COLUMN age;
```

5.3 Data Manipulation Language

5.3.1 Updates

The `INSERT` statement allows the insertion of one t-uple given by its values or of a set of t-uples defined by the result of a query on existing tables. It is possible to give a list of attributes if we need or want to change the order of values from the one implied by the table declaration or if some values are omitted (provided they can be padded with null or default values).

The following two expressions define the general syntax of the `INSERT` statement.

```
INSERT INTO table_name [(attribute_name [,attribute_name]*)]
VALUES (value [,value]*);

INSERT INTO table_name [(attribute_name [,attribute_name]*)]
query;
```

The first expression defines the insertion of a t-uple. The second expression defines the insertion of the result of a query. We can, for instance, create a new entry for the employee John McMallen, living at 107 Jln Kampung Baru.

```
INSERT INTO employee (address, employee_name)
VALUES ('107 Jln Kampung Baru', 'John McMallen');
```

Notice the use of single quotes for strings, which is the traditional syntax for SQL strings although most database management systems now accept double quotes.

We can also, for instance, insert a new entry for the employee Hui Cheng whose address is not given and will take the default value `'company address'` if it has been declared or a null value if authorised.

Section 5.3. Data Manipulation Language

```
INSERT INTO employee (employee_name) VALUES ('Hui Cheng');
```

Instead of the view **manager** we defined in the previous section, let us create an actual table **manager** and populate it with the names and addresses of all the employees who are managers of some departments. We first create the table.

```
CREATE TABLE manager
  (manager_name VARCHAR(24) PRIMARY KEY,
   address VARCHAR(48),
   department_name VARCHAR(24));
```

Then we populate the table with the result of a query on the tables **employee** and **department**.

```
INSERT INTO manager (manager_name, address, department_name)
SELECT employee.employee_name, employee.address,
       department.department_name
FROM employee, department
WHERE employee.employee_name = department.manager;
```

Notice that subsequent updates to the underlying tables are not propagated to the table **manager**.

T-uples verifying a given property can be deleted from a table. The property or qualification takes the syntax of the WHERE clause of queries as we present in the next section. The following expression defines the general syntax of a DELETE statement.

```
DELETE
FROM table_name
[WHERE qualification];
```

It is, for instance, possible to delete all the departments located at 22 Bukit Ridge from the table **department**.

```
DELETE
FROM department
WHERE location = '22 Bukit Ridge';
```

Similarly, individual attributes of t-uples verifying a given property can be updated. In addition, the assignment used to define the new value for the attribute can refer to the old value of the attribute in the expression on the right hand side of the assignment. The following expression defines the general syntax of an UPDATE statement.

```
UPDATE table_name
SET attribute_name = expression
[WHERE qualification];
```

For instance, the following statement increases the budget of the departments managed by John McMallen by 50%. Incidentally, it happens that there is only one such department since we imposed a unique constraint that guarantees that a manager is in charge of one department only. However, in general, updates concern sets of t-uples.

```
UPDATE department
SET budget = budget * 1.5
WHERE manager = 'John McMallen';
```

Finally, sets of updates can be grouped into transactions. In general, SQL transactions begin implicitly and end with the process that executes them (then they attempt to commit unless they are aborted and rolled back by the database management system) or they are explicitly started with the START TRANSACTION command and ended, committed or aborted, by the programmer using one of the two commands: COMMIT and ROLLBACK, respectively. Additional details about the programming of transactions can be found in Chapter 6.

5.3.2 Simple Queries

A simple SQL query is composed of two or three main clauses. The SELECT clause contains the list of attributes or expressions defining what is kept in the resulting table. The FROM clause contains the list of tables being queried. The WHERE clause, which is optional, contains a condition to be verified by t-uples of the tables involved in order to contribute to the result. Each clause is indicated by the corresponding keyword. The order of the SELECT, FROM, WHERE and other clauses (we present later GROUP BY, HAVING and ORDER BY) must be respected. The following expression defines the general syntax of a simple query statement.

```
SELECT target_list
FROM table_list
[WHERE qualification];
```

In the following query, the keyword * in the SELECT clause indicates that all the attributes from the tables involved must be kept. There is no WHERE clause, therefore all t-uples participate in the result. The FROM clause indicates a single table. This query simply prints all the t-uples in the table employee.

```
SELECT *
FROM employee;
```

If we are interested in listing only the names of the managers and the locations of the departments in the table department, we can use the following query.

```
SELECT manager, location
FROM department;
```

It is possible to add a condition in the WHERE clause. For instance, we may want to list the names of the managers and the names of the departments for those departments whose budget is below $1000000.

```
SELECT manager, location
FROM department
WHERE budget < 1000000;
```

If the query involves several tables, the condition also allows the appropriate combination of t-uples of the different tables involved. Notice that attributes can be qualified using the table name and the dot notation in order to avoid ambiguities. The following query prints the names of the employees together with the locations of the departments for which the employees work.

```
SELECT employee.employee_name, department.manager
FROM employee, work_for, department
WHERE employee.employee_name = work_for.employee_name
AND work_for.department_name = department.department_name;
```

In order to simplify the writing of such long queries, aliases, also called correlation names, can be given to the tables involved. The following query is the same as the previous query in which the tables: `employee`, `work_for` and `department` are given the aliases e, w and d, respectively.

```
SELECT e.employee_name, d.manager
FROM employee e, work_for w, department d
WHERE e.employee_name = w.employee_name
AND w.department_name = d.department_name;
```

Elements of the list in the SELECT clause can also be renamed for printing purposes. The keyword AS is used. In the following query we rename the attribute `employee_name` as `employee` and the attribute `manager` as `boss`.

```
SELECT e.employee_name AS employee, d.manager AS boss
FROM employee e, work_for w, department d
WHERE e.employee_name = w.employee_name
AND w.department_name = d.department_name;
```

Aliases are necessary when the query requires several copies of one table. They allow the programmer to distinguish between the different instances of that table. The following query prints the pairs of names of distinct departments located at the same address.

```
SELECT d1.department_name AS department1,
       d2.department_name AS department2
FROM department d1, department d2
WHERE d1.location = d2.location
AND d1.department_name <> d2.department_name;
```

Notice the renaming in the SELECT clause.

Let us now consider the following query, which prints the names of employees working for a department together with the location of the department.

Section 5.3. Data Manipulation Language

```
SELECT e.employee_name, d.location
FROM employee e, work_for w, department d
WHERE e.employee_name = w.employee_name
AND w.department_name = d.department_name;
```

Since an employee could work for several departments and since these departments could be located at the same address, the name of the employee and the location could be printed several times in the result of the query. Indeed, the relational model as implemented by SQL differs from the theoretical model we have seen. It has a bag-semantics instead of the set-semantics we have studied. Tables differ from relations in that they may contain duplicates. They are bags or multi-sets and not sets. To avoid duplicates in the result of queries we can use the keyword **DISTINCT**. The following query lists unique pairs of employee names and department locations.

```
SELECT DISTINCT e.employee_name, d.location
FROM employee e, work_for w, department d
WHERE e.employee_name = w.employee_name
AND w.department_name = d.department_name;
```

Such queries are called Project-Select-Join (PSJ) queries. Indeed, their semantics is given by an expression of relational algebra that involves a projection, a selection and a Cartesian product. The standard semantics of the above query is given by the following relational algebra expression.

$$\pi_{(employee.employee\_name, department.location)}(\\
\sigma_{employee.employee\_name=work\_for.employee\_name \\ \land work\_for.department\_name=department.department\_name} \\
(employee \times work\_for \times department)).$$

Notice, however, that the choice of keywords for SQL might be confusing since the **SELECT** clause defines the projection list while the θ-condition of the selection is given in the **WHERE** clause!

SQL is a concrete language derived from t-uple relation calculus. The one to one correspondence between the respective syntactic constructs can be discovered by comparing the SQL query above to the following t-uple relational calculus query. The comparison is left as an exercise to the reader.

$$\{t \mid \exists e \in employee \exists w \in work\_for \exists d \in department$$
$$(e.employee\_name = w.employee\_name$$
$$\land w.department\_name = d.department\_name$$
$$\land t.employee\_name = e.employee\_name$$
$$\land t.location = d.location)\}$$

It can even be said that SQL implements a list-semantics if we consider the additional clause `ORDER BY` that allows the printing of the result of a query in a specified order. For instance, the following query prints the names of the employees together with the locations of the departments for which the employees work in ascending alphabetical order of the employee names and in descending alphabetical order of the locations.

```
SELECT employee.employee_name, department.manager
FROM employee, work_for, department
WHERE employee.employee_name = work_for.employee_name
AND work_for.department_name = department.department_name
ORDER BY employee.employee_name ASC, department.location DESC;
```

The keyword `ASC` can be omitted since it is the default order for attributes listed in the `ORDER BY` clause.

SQL also allows arithmetic expression in both the `SELECT` and `WHERE` clauses (and also in the `HAVING` clause used for expressing conditions involving aggregate functions that we present below).

For example, the following query prints for each department, the name of its manager, its location and its budget multiplied by a factor of 1.5.

```
SELECT manager, location, budget * 1.5
FROM department
WHERE budget < 1000000;
```

The following query prints for each department whose budget, although increased by 50%, is still below $1000000, the name of its manager and its location.

Section 5.3. Data Manipulation Language
67

```
SELECT manager, location
FROM department
WHERE budget * 1.5 < 1000000;
```

5.3.3 Aggregate Queries

Most database applications involve computing functions of sets of values in one or more columns of a table. Typically, we may need to count t-uples in a table or to compute the sum, minimum, average or other statistics over the set of values in the column of a table. Such functions are called *aggregate* functions. SQL includes constructs to express such functions in the queries. The functions COUNT, count, SUM, summation, MIN, minimum, MAX, maximum and AVG, average, are the standard aggregate functions available in SQL. Queries involving such functions are called aggregate queries.

The following query counts the number of t-uples in the table department.

```
SELECT COUNT(*)
FROM department;
```

The following query counts the number of values in the table department. It is equivalent to the previous query.

```
SELECT COUNT(location)
FROM department;
```

Yet values may appear several times in the column location since several departments may be located at the same address. In order to count the distinct locations, we need to add the keyword DISTINCT in front of the argument of the count function, as illustrated by the following query.

```
SELECT COUNT(DISTINCT location)
FROM department;
```

The keyword ALL, conversely expresses explicitly that all values including duplicate values should be counted. It is the default. The following expression is an example.

```
SELECT COUNT(ALL location)
FROM department;
```

Aggregate functions can be computed for sub-groups of t-uples agreeing on certain attributes. The list of attributes on which the t-uples need to agree is indicated in an additional **GROUP BY** clause. For instance, the following query computes the average budget for each location, i.e., it prints, for each location, the average of all the budgets of the departments at the same location.

```
SELECT AVG(budget)
FROM department
GROUP BY location;
```

It is, in this case, also possible to print the location (but attributes that do not appear in the **GROUP BY** clause cannot be printed).

```
SELECT location, AVG(budget)
FROM department
GROUP BY location;
```

Several aggregate functions can be used in the same query. It is possible to print the location, average and biggest budget at each location and to count the number of departments at the same location.

```
SELECT location, AVG(budget), MAX(budget),
       COUNT(DISTINCT department_name)
FROM department
GROUP BY location;
```

Notice that the DISTINCT keyword is unnecessary in the above query for our particular example since the name of a department is a primary key. Similarly, aggregate functions are unnecessary in the following query.

```
SELECT location, department_name, AVG(budget)
FROM department
GROUP BY location, department_name;
```

References in the **SELECT** clause can only be made to aggregates and to attributes in the **GROUP BY** clause. Therefore, the following query is incorrect and will be rejected by the SQL parser.

Section 5.3. Data Manipulation Language   69

```
SELECT location, AVG(budget)
FROM department;
```

Finally, aggregate functions can also be used to express conditions. Yet they cannot be used in the **WHERE** clause. The following query, aiming at printing the locations at which the average departmental budget is above $2000000, is incorrect.

```
SELECT location
FROM department
WHERE AVG(budget) > 2000000
GROUP BY location;
```

SQL requires that such conditions involving aggregates be expressed in the special **HAVING** clause. Thus, the above query must be rewritten as follows (notice that the **HAVING** clause must be after the **GROUP BY** clause).

```
SELECT location
FROM department
GROUP BY location
HAVING AVG(budget) > 2000000;
```

5.3.4 Nested Queries

The result of an SQL query is a table. It seems therefore natural to use the results of one or more queries, which we then call sub-queries, to formulate other queries. This can be done if we create a table and populate it with the results of the sub-query. We can then use the new table to express the query. This can also be done if we define a view as the sub-query. We can then use the view to express the query.

Yet SQL allows, in some cases, the sub-query to be expressed directly inside the query. We examine now the use of sub-queries, also called nested queries, in the **WHERE** and **HAVING** clauses of an SQL query.

Nested queries can be introduced by =, <, >, **LIKE** etc., if they return a singleton containing a t-uple with a single attribute (i.e., if they return a single value). To ensure it is the case is mostly the responsibility of the user, as sometimes it can only be checked by the database management system at runtime, to guarantee that the query returns a single value. The above operators can be combined with NOT. The following query prints the location and average budget of departments at the same location such that this average budget is strictly bigger than the average budget over all departments.

```
SELECT location, AVG(d1.budget)
FROM department d1
GROUP BY location
HAVING AVG(d1.budget) > (
  SELECT AVG(d2.budget)
  FROM department d2);
```

Nested queries can be introduced by ALL, ANY, IN, EXISTS if they return a table. The above operators can be combined with NOT.

ALL and ANY are combined with =, <, > etc. ALL and ANY are quantifiers, respectively for all and exists. ALL requires that the comparison holds for all values in the set defined by the sub-query. ANY requires that the comparison holds for any value in the set defined by the sub-query. Sub-queries preceded by ALL or ANY must return sets of t-uples with a single attribute.

The following query prints the names of the employees working for a department located at 22 Raffles Street.

```
SELECT employee_name
FROM work_for
WHERE department_name = ANY (
  SELECT department_name
  FROM department
  WHERE location = '22 Raffles Street');
```

The following query prints the names of the employees working for a department not located at 22 Raffles Street.

```
SELECT employee_name
FROM work_for
WHERE department_name <> ALL (
  SELECT department_name
```

Section 5.3. Data Manipulation Language

```
  FROM department
  WHERE location = '22 Raffles Street');
```

IN is used to test the belonging of a value to a set defined by a sub-query. Sub-queries preceded by IN must return sets of t-uples with a single attribute. The following query prints the names of the employees working for a department located at 22 Raffles Street.

```
SELECT employee_name
FROM work_for
WHERE department_name IN (
  SELECT department_name
  FROM department
  WHERE location = '22 Raffles Street');
```

EXISTS is used to test whether the result of a sub-query is empty. The following query prints the names of employees living at an address that is also the location of a department.

```
SELECT employee_name
FROM employee
WHERE EXISTS (
  SELECT *
  FROM department
  WHERE address = location);
```

For this latter query, we have used the opportunity to reference an attribute of the outer query in the sub-query. A reference to attribute can only be used within the clauses (SELECT, WHERE, HAVING etc.) in the query where it is defined or within recursively nested queries. For instance, the following query is incorrect, since the attribute d2.budget cannot leave the scope of the nested query.

```
SELECT location, AVG(d1.budget), AVG(d2.budget)
FROM department d1
GROUP BY location
HAVING AVG(d1.budget) > (
```

```
    SELECT AVG(d2.budget)
    FROM department d2);
```

In theory, queries can be nested at any arbitrary level. There can be nested queries in the nested queries. Yet, most database management systems impose a maximum depth of nesting for (bad) reasons related to implementation and performance of the query optimiser.

Nested queries sometimes increase the readability of queries. They also increase the expressive power of SQL. However, nested queries should be used with care since, in practice, they make the optimisation of queries more complicated for the database management system and may result in less efficient evaluations. We leave to the reader the exercise of finding examples (possibly among the above queries) of nested queries that cannot be rewritten as simple queries.

Chapter 6
SQL and Programming Languages

6.1 Motivation

SQL is a language for defining and manipulating data in a relational database. However, SQL alone is not sufficient to program an entire application. Indeed, by design, it is neither *computationally complete* nor *system complete*.

By computational completeness we mean the ability to express in the language all theoretically possible computations. In order to allow database management systems to optimise effectively the queries declaratively expressed by the programmers, a query language in general and SQL in particular is preferably limited to a subset of what a general programming language could express. Evidently, many examples of programs that cannot be written in SQL can be given. Let us consider an example that illustrates things that cannot be done in SQL-92 but can be done in SQL-99 and things that cannot be done in SQL-99 but may very well be possible in a subsequent version of the standard.

Let us consider for example a relation *flight* with the following scheme.

$flight($ $flight\_number,$
             $departure\_time,$
             $arrival\_time,$
             $origin,$
             $destination).$

It is used to store basic flight information in the information system of a flight reservation system and contains flights data from all airlines, origins and destination airports. Listing the destinations reachable from Singapore in one or more hops is not possible in SQL-92 as it requires to iteratively (or recursively) join the table *flight* with itself or with the result of the previous iterations until all the possible destinations have been found. Such an iteration or recursion is possible in SQL-99. Computing the actual shortest path (for instance, in the number of connections) between two airports involves: recursion or iteration, aggregation and the building of a complex result in the form of a list (transit points in order). This is not possible in today's SQL standard.

By system completeness (sometimes called *resource completeness*) we mean the ability to express in the language operations involving communication with the computer's operating system and, through it, with the computer's hardware and peripherals. SQL does not contain constructs to, for example, write in a file, print on a printer or more generally build a user interface as needed by most applications.

Based on the previous considerations, it follows that most if not all database applications require a program in which SQL and a general purpose programming language cooperate. SQL provides optimised access to the data in the database and the programming language provides system completeness.

In this chapter, we examine how SQL and a programming language can be coupled and cooperate. SQL can be coupled with programming languages in several different ways:

- *Internal coupling.* SQL is extended with further programming constructs (for instance, procedural constructs such as procedure and function definitions, variables and control structures). The extended language can then be used as a traditional programming language inside the database management system and the defined procedure and functions called by the programmer.

- *External coupling.* An existing programming language, such as the $Java^{TM}$[1] or the C language, is coupled with SQL. The main code of applications based on this approach is run outside the database management system.

From the programmer's viewpoint there are two major forms of external coupling:

---

[1] $Java^{TM}$ and all $Java^{TM}$-based marks are trademarks or registered trademarks of Sun Microsystems, Inc.

Section 6.1. Motivation   75

1. *Database connectivity.* A standard set of primitives is available within
   the programming language. These primitives interface the programming language and the database management system allowing connection and execution of statements from the programming language. Two commonly used standardised interfaces are: the *Object DataBase Connectivity* (ODBC) interface commonly used for interfacing C or Visual Basic applications with database management systems, and the *Java DataBase Connectivity* JDBC^{TM2} interface for interfacing Java^{TM} applications with database management systems.

2. *Embedded SQL.* SQL commands are embedded directly in an extended version of a programming language. Usually a pre-processor or a compiler translates the program with embedded SQL into a program in the host language with remote calls to the database in a standard or proprietary database connectivity model.

In practice, most applications combine both internal and external couplings.

Regardless of the coupling approach, interactions between a programming language and the database management system involves the following steps for each SQL statement:

- preparation of the statement;

- execution of the statement;

- collection of the results.

The preparation of a statement consists of the construction of data structures necessary for communication with the database management system and possibly the compilation and optimisation of the statement by the database management system. We can distinguish two main ways in which a particular coupling approach prepares the SQL statements: it can require *static SQL statements* or allow *dynamic SQL statements*. A static SQL statement must be written in the program source (although some of it such as scalar

---
[2]JDBC^{TM} is a trademark of Sun Microsystems, Inc.

values can be parameterised). A dynamic SQL statement can be built entirely at runtime. Obviously, dynamic statements raise difficult optimisation, compilation and evaluation issues for both the database and the host language. One can expect static statements to be more efficient. Some coupling approaches allow static statements only.

The execution or evaluation of INSERT, DELETE and UPDATE statements, as well as DDL statements, usually returns some value (a number) or data structure representing either the number of inserted/deleted/modified t-uples or the details of the successful or erroneous completion of the operation. The result of the evaluation of a SELECT statement is a set of t-uples. If the size of this result is sufficiently small for the entire set of t-uples to fit into main memory, the obvious and intuitive solution is to cast the set of t-uples into a table (or a scalar if the result contains a single value). If the size of the result is unknown, or too big to be efficiently loaded or to fit into main memory, a *cursor* mechanism allows the programmer to fetch individual t-uples one at a time, while the result is kept in the database. Informally, a cursor is a pointer to one of the t-uples in a result held by the database management system. A cursor is therefore associated with an evaluation of a query. At any time the t-uple a cursor points at, or some of the values of the attributes of this t-uple, can be fetched and cast into a data structure of the host language (vector, array, scalar etc.). Functions or methods associated with a cursor allow the programmer to control the movement of the cursor in the result, i.e., moving to the next, previous, first or last t-uple in the result. Cursors are usually opened and closed explicitly.

In addition to the above interactions, externally coupled solutions need to preliminarily and explicitly establish a connection with the database management system and the required database. Similarly, at the end of the process, the connection with the database management system should be terminated. Connections are said to be opened and closed, respectively.

Finally, all coupling approaches require some implicit and possibly explicit definition of the transactional units. Transaction blocks are sometimes explicitly defined and their ending, committing or rolling back, programmed. This is usually done in association with an exception handling mechanism to see to anomalies in the execution of the host language statements or of the SQL statements. The programming of exception handling in programming languages is never an easy task. It is particularly difficult when the language is coupled with a database management system since the notion of transaction in the database management system must be taken into account.

In the following, the three main coupling approaches are discussed in further details. To illustrate, we use two tables as defined by the following SQL statements.

```
CREATE TABLE employee
  (name VARCHAR(24) PRIMARY KEY,
   address VARCHAR(36) DEFAULT 'company address',
   department VARCHAR(24) REFERENCES department(name),
   salary NUMERIC);

CREATE TABLE department
  (name VARCHAR(24) PRIMARY KEY,
   location VARCHAR(36),
   budget NUMERIC);
```

6.2 Procedural SQL

Most database management systems support a procedural extension of SQL. The programs are organised in routines, i.e., procedures and functions. The routines are executed by the database management system. They can be called either directly from within the database management system or from externally coupled applications. Unfortunately, no standard procedural extension of SQL exists. However, the new SQL-99 standard establishes how SQL routines can be defined and invoked. In the following, we describe how manipulation, transaction and exception handling, and stored procedures and functions can be programmed. We discuss the PL/SQL^{TM}[3] procedural extension of SQL for the Oracle 9i^{TM}[4] database.

---

[3]PL/SQL^{TM} is a trademark of Oracle Corporation
[4]Oracle 9i^{TM} is a trademark of Oracle Corporation.

6.2.1 Manipulation

Any program written by using an SQL procedural extension is typically composed of at least two distinct parts: a declaration part and an execution part. No specific connection to the database management system is required since the program can only be executed directly from within the database management system.

The declaration part contains type declarations for all the variables used in the program. Any SQL type can be used for this purpose. Default values and NOT NULL constraints can also be specified. In the PL/SQL^{TM} syntax, the declaration part starts with the keyword DECLARE. The following is an example of a declaration part in the PL/SQL^{TM} syntax.

```
DECLARE
  salary NUMERIC NOT NULL;
  credit_bound  NUMERIC := 3000000;
  date DATE;
  employee_number NUMERIC := 0;
  manager BOOLEAN;
```

The execution section is usually identified by specific block constructs, such as the keywords BEGIN END around the block in the PL/SQL^{TM} syntax, and contains both typical procedural constructs and SQL statements. SQL statements and procedural code communicate via previously declared variables. Such variables can be used in the WHERE part of a SELECT, DELETE and UPDATE statement, in the SET part of an UPDATE statement and in the VALUES part of an INSERT statement. The variables replace constants in the SQL statements. In the following example, a variable my_department_name of type VARCHAR is used to hold the name of the department, sales. We print the names of the employess of the sales department.

```
DECLARE
my_department_name VARCHAR;
BEGIN
  my_department_name := 'sales';
  SELECT name
```

Section 6.2. Procedural SQL

```
    FROM employee
    WHERE department = my_department_name;
END;
```

If the SQL statement necessarily returns a single t-uple the `SELECT INTO` statement can be used to insert the t-uple values inside variables. In the following example, the program assigns the value of the salary of Nancy Santi to the variable `my_salary`.

```
DECLARE
  my_salary NUMERIC;
BEGIN
  SELECT salary INTO my_salary WHERE name = 'Nancy Santi';
END;
```

SQL procedural extensions support typical control structures and constructs, such as conditionals (*if-then-else*-statements) and iterations (*for-*, *until-* and *while-* loops) in one syntactic form or another.

The following example illustrates the usage of conditional construct in the PL/SQL^{TM} syntax. In the following example, the program inserts into the database the name, address and salary of a new employee of the research department. The salary of this employee is computed according to some sales figures. The details of the computation of the sales figure are not given (this part of the program is replaced in the following listing by '[...]').

```
DECLARE
  sales NUMERIC;
  sal NUMERIC;
BEGIN
[...]
IF sales > 50000 THEN sal := 1500;
ELSIF sales > 35000 THEN sal := 1200;
ELSE sal := 1000;
END IF;
INSERT INTO employee
VALUES ('Tiziana Dezza', '132, via Dellatti', 'research', sal);
END;
```

We present later an example of an iteration control structure for the illustration of the use of cursors.

When the execution of a (SELECT) statement returns a set of t-uples, a cursor must be used to fetch t-uples one at the time. The cursor is declared by specifying its name and the statement it is associated with. This is done in the declaration section. For example, the following program chunk declares a cursor named `high_budget` associated with a query finding all departments having a budget greater than $10000.

```
CURSOR high_budget IS
  SELECT name, budget
  FROM department
  WHERE budget > 10000;
```

Usually, cursor declarations only associate a cursor to a query. The query is executed when the cursor is explicitly activated in the execution section. The cursor is said to be opened. This is done in the PL/SQL^{TM} syntax with the OPEN statement as shown in the following example.

```
OPEN high_budget;
```

Once the cursor is opened, it initially points before the first t-uple of the result table (and not at the first t-uple). The values of the attributes of the t-uple pointed at can be fetched into variables. In the PL/SQL^{TM} syntax this is done using the FETCH INTO statement. The general syntax for fetching result t-uples is the following.

```
FETCH [orientation] FROM cursor_name
INTO variable_list;
```

In the above command, `orientation` is optional. It indicates how the cursor has to be moved on the result set before the values are fetched. Its default value is NEXT, reading the t-uple following the current cursor position. Other possible values are PRIOR, moving the cursor to the preceding t-uple, FIRST, moving to the first t-uple, LAST, moving to the last t-uple of the result set, ABSOLUTE n, moving to the nth t-uple starting from the beginning of the result set, and RELATIVE n moving to the nth t-uple starting from the

Section 6.2. Procedural SQL

current position. For example, the following statement fetches the next t-uple associated with cursor `high_budget`, and inserts the values of the attributes of this t-uple into two previously declared variables `name` and `budget`.

```
FETCH NEXT FROM high_budget
INTO name, budget;
```

A cursor is associated with a Boolean variable `NOTFOUND`. This variable is true when the cursor has reached the first or last t-uple and is moved backward or forward, respectively.

When the necessary fetching is finished, the cursor activation is terminated by using the `CLOSE` statement. The cursor is said to be closed.

The following code is typical of the standard processing of the result of a query. Notice that, since SQL procedural extensions are system complete, typical read and write command are usually supported. We use a `dbmsoutput.put_line` command to display the result of the query.

```
DECLARE
name VARCHAR(24);
budget NUMERIC;
CURSOR high_budget IS
  SELECT name, budget
  FROM department
  WHERE budget > 10000;
BEGIN
OPEN high_budget;
LOOP
  FETCH NEXT FROM high_budget
  INTO name, budget;
  EXIT WHEN high_budget%NOTFOUND;
  dbmsoutput.put_line('Name: '|| name);
  dbmsoutput.put_line(' Budget: '|| budget);
END LOOP;
CLOSE high_budget;
END;
```

All the examples presented above are static SQL statements. However, dynamic SQL statements can be executed in some SQL procedural extensions. The following PL/SQL command executes a dynamic statement. `dynamic_statement` is a variable or string that contains the SQL statement to be executed. The string could have been constructed at runtime.

```
EXECUTE IMMEDIATE dynamic_statement;
```

6.2.2 Transactions and Exception Handling

SQL procedural extensions support statements for defining transactional mechanisms. In the PL/SQL^{TM} syntax, the first SQL statement of a program execution implicitly starts a transaction, which is ended and committed at the end of the program execution unless stated otherwise. However, transactions can be explicitly ended using the transaction ending constructs `COMMIT` or `ROLLBACK`. Since there is no `BEGIN TRANSACTION` construct in the PL/SQL^{TM} syntax, a new transaction starts implicitly after the ending, commit or rollback, of a transaction.

Procedural SQL extension usually supports two types of exceptions: *system exceptions*, directly raised by the system, and *user exceptions*, defined in the program and raised by the program. When an exception is raised, a specific code is executed, which has been specified in a special section of the execution part of the program starting with the construct `EXCEPTION`. The program continues normally after the exception code has been executed. In the following example, the sum of the budgets assigned to all the departments is computed and, if it is equal to zero, thus no budget has been assigned yet, a user exception is raised. Then the total budget is divided by the number of employees. In this latter case, if there is no employee in the database, a system exception is raised in order to avoid a division by zero.

```
DECLARE
  sum_bud NUMERIC;
  avg_bud NUMERIC;
BEGIN
  SELECT SUM(budget) INTO sum_bud FROM department;
  IF sum_bud = 0  THEN RAISE ZERO_BUDGET END IF;
```

Section 6.2. Procedural SQL   83

```
    SELECT sum_bud/COUNT(*) INTO avg_bud FROM employee;
    EXCEPTION
      WHEN ZERO_DIVIDE
          THEN PRINT "Division by Zero";
      WHEN ZERO_BUDGET
          THEN PRINT "No budget has been assigned yet";
END;
```

Several system exceptions can be raised that correspond to anomalies in the interaction with the database management system. These exceptions are very useful. The most useful are probably the exceptions that are raised when updates violate integrity constraints. For instance, the exception `dup_val_on_index` is raised in the PL/SQL^{TM} syntax when there is an attempt to enter two t-uples with the same primary key.

6.2.3 Stored Procedures and Functions

The programs written in SQL procedural extensions are both executed and stored by the database management system. In this section, we look at the syntax for defining and manipulating such procedures and functions. These routines are usually referred to as *stored procedures* and *stored functions* respectively or, as in the respective SQL standard mentioning them, *invoked routines*.

Similarly to procedures and functions defined in any programming language, SQL routines facilitate software development since they help the programmer to factorise her code. They also help improve knowledge independence since they are stored and managed by the database management system and can be shared and reused by several programmers while the access to their source is controlled.

According to the SQL-99 standard an SQL routine consists of at least three items: a routine name, a set of parameter declarations and a routine body. The routine body can be written in various programming languages, including the database management system's proprietary procedural SQL extension. In the following, procedures and functions are illustrated by using the PL/SQL^{TM} procedural extension.

Procedures can be created by using the CREATE PROCEDURE DDL statement, that in SQL-99 has the following basic structure.

```
CREATE PROCEDURE procedure_name
( SQL_parameter_list )
procedure_body
```

The SQL_parameter_list is a list of SQL variable declarations, as specified in the CREATE TABLE statement, plus a parameter mode, which can be IN (the default value), if the parameter value is only read; OUT, if the parameter value is only written or INOUT, if the parameter value is both read and written.

The following example illustrates the creation of a procedure to raise the salary of a certain employee, whose name and amount of increase are provided as input. The body of the procedure, here omitted and replaced by [...], follows the keyword IS.

```
CREATE PROCEDURE
    raise_salary (emp_name INTEGER, amount NUMERIC) IS [...]
```

According to the SQL-99 standard for stored procedures the procedure is invoked using the keyword CALL. Yet, in the PL/SQL^{TM} syntax, the keyword CALL is not used. The following illustrates the invocation of a procedure in SQL-99 where p1,...,pn are variables, constants or terms that can be evaluated. The type of the variables, constants and terms must comply with the type of the corresponding parameter as declared in the CREATE PROCEDURE statement.

```
CALL procedure_name(p1,...,pn);
```

For example, the following is a procedure call in the PL/SQL^{TM} syntax to raise the salary of Eva Aiello by $50.

```
raise_salary('Eva Aiello',50);
```

Similarly, according to the SQL-99 standard, functions can be created by using the CREATE FUNCTION DDL statement. The following is the generic syntax for a function declaration in which datatype is the type of the value

Section 6.2. Procedural SQL

to be returned, and `SQL_parameter_list` and `function_body` have the same meaning as similar constructs in the CREATE PROCEDURE statement.

```
CREATE FUNCTION function_name ( SQL_parameter_list )
RETURN datatype
function_body
```

The following example illustrates the creation of a function whose body is again omitted. We assume the function computes and returns the average salary of the employees in the department whose name is given as a parameter.

```
CREATE FUNCTION
   avg_salary (department VARCHAR(24)) RETURN NUMERIC IS [...]
```

A function call can be present in any place where a value of the function return type appears. No keyword is required in this case. The following illustrates the invocation of a function in SQL-99 where p1,...,pn are variables, constants or terms that can be evaluated. The type of the variables, constants and terms must comply with the type of the corresponding parameter as declared in the CREATE FUNCTION statement. The result is likely to be assigned to a variable as is with normal functions.

```
function_name(p1,...,pn);
```

For example, the following is a function call in the PL/SQL^{TM} syntax that returns the average salary in the research department.

```
avg_salary('research');
```

6.2.4 Example

The following is a complete example of a procedure in the PL/SQL^{TM} syntax. The procedure computes the average salary in the **employee** table and increases the salaries of all employees by 5% if the average salary is less than $1000. It decreases all the salaries by 5% otherwise. Then the names and salaries of the employees working in a department whose name is given as input to the procedure are printed.

```
CREATE PROCEDURE Modify_salary (my_department VARCHAR) AS
DECLARE
      avg_sal NUMERIC;

      my_name VARCHAR;
      my_salary NUMERIC;
      CURSOR Name_Salary_cr IS
         SELECT name,salary
         FROM employee
         WHERE department = my_department;
BEGIN
      SELECT AVG(salary) INTO avg_sal FROM employee;
      IF (avg_sal < 1000) THEN
         UPDATE employee SET salary = salary*1,05;
      ELSE
         UPDATE employee SET salary = salary*0,95;
      END IF

      LOOP
        FETCH NEXT FROM Name_Salary_cr INTO  my_name,my_salary;
        EXIT WHEN Name_Salary_cr%NOTFOUND;
        dbmsoutput.put_line('Name: '|| my_name);
        dbmsoutput.put_line('  Salary: '|| my_salary);
      END LOOP;
END
```

6.3 Database Connectivity

In the database connectivity approach, the access to a database in a database management system is done through a programming interface called the *Call Level Interface* or CLI. The CLI is implemented by a library for the host language and communicates with the database management system with a protocol implemented by a driver on the host language side and a server on the database management system side.

Section 6.3. Database Connectivity

Most commercial database management systems offer a particular database connectivity solution. There have been several attempts to standardise these solutions. SQL-99 specifies how CLIs must be defined while major database connectivity approaches become *de facto* standards. As mentioned before, the two main standard database connectivity solutions are the ODBC interface and JDBC^{TM} interface. Both libraries support almost the same functionalities even if the JDBC^{TM} syntax may appear simpler than the ODBC syntax.

Most commercial database management systems are compatible with the main CLIs, the ODBC and JDBC^{TM} CLI. Both ODBC and JDBC^{TM} drivers (see Section 6.3.1) are available for those database management systems.

The usage of standard CLIs guarantees a high level of portability of the application from one database management system to another. It also enables interoperability with several database management systems since the database connectivity solutions are designed to allow an application to connect to multiple, possibly heterogeneous, backend systems (incidentally and beyond the scope of this section, the backend systems need not be database managements systems!).

In the following, we first introduce the reference architecture for database connectivity approaches. Then, we describe how connection, manipulation, transaction and exception handling can be programmed. We choose to discuss the JDBC^{TM} solution.

6.3.1 The Database Connectivity Reference Architecture

The database connectivity generic reference architecture is presented in Figure 6.1. It is the architecture of both ODBC and JDBC^{TM} applications.

The information flow of the application follows the typical flow presented in Section 6.1. During the execution of the main application program, a library function call is captured by the *Driver Manager* located on the machine running the program and to which the program has been explicitly or implicitly connected depending on the operating system. The Driver Manager dispatches the calls to the appropriate driver connected to the database management system to which the call is directed. The Driver Manager, as mentioned before, allows the connectivity with several database management

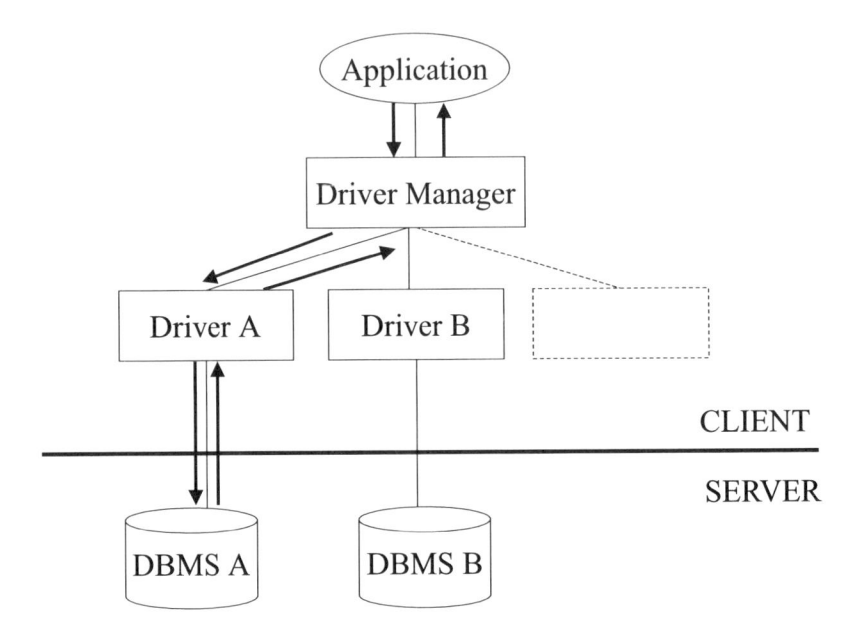

Figure 6.1: The Database Connectivity Reference Architecture

systems. It is the application that indicates which drivers it requires and to which driver a call is targeted.

The driver is capable of dynamically connecting to the database management system. It understands its communication protocol. It is also in charge of the translation of the calls into requests to the database system specific syntax and of their transmission.

The database management system receives the requests directly from the driver, executes the SQL statements and returns back results.

The driver is also in charge of the collection, translation into the CLI standard and transmission of the results.

The driver and the Driver Manager conceal from the application the heterogeneity of the languages and protocols of the database management systems. Note that the application does not communicate with the driver but only with the Driver Manager component.

In the rest of this section, we illustrate the different aspects of program-

Section 6.3. Database Connectivity

ming with a JDBC^{TM} CLI. The JDBC^{TM} definition was developed in 1996 as a database connectivity solution for Java^{TM} programming allowing pure Java^{TM} database applications. The JDBC^{TM} interface is a Java^{TM} API, containing one class or interface for each main database connectivity concept. More precisely, the JDBC^{TM} API contains only one class, corresponding to the Driver Manager. All other components, for example, the driver, are interfaces. Loading a driver thus means loading specific classes implementing a given JDBC^{TM} interface.

Four types of JDBC^{TM} drivers can be identified. They differ in the level of indirection used to communicate with the database management system. Type 1 drivers, also called JDBC^{TM}-ODBC bridges, translate JDBC^{TM} calls into ODBC calls to an ODBC driver of the database management system. Type 2 drivers, also called native drivers, translate JDBC^{TM} calls into calls to native drivers of the database management system. Type 3 drivers, also called JDBC^{TM} middleware, are Java^{TM} middleware gateways to the database management system. Type 4 drivers, simply called JDBC^{TM} drivers, provide direct access to the database management system server, without using intermediate software.

6.3.2 Connection

As explained in Section 6.1, the first step for a program using an external coupling approach is establishing a connection with the database management system. The programmer must indicate the driver to be used and request it be loaded. Each driver, i.e., normally a specific driver of a given type for a particular database management system, corresponds to a Java^{TM} class. The class name is usually provided with the database manager documentation. In the case of a JDBC^{TM}-ODBC driver, however, the driver is generic since it can communicate with any ODBC driver. The following excerpt of the Java^{TM} code loads a type 1 driver.

```
Class.forName("sun.jdbc.odbc.JdbcOdbcDriver");
```

After loading the driver, a connection with the database management system is established. The database management system must be univocally identified through a resource locator of the following form, in which

`<subprotocol>` identifies the driver to be used and `<subname>` identifies the specific database to be connected with.

jdbc: `<subprotocol>`: `<subname>`

If a type 1 driver is used, the resource locator has the following form.

jdbc:odbc:`<subname>`

In general, the connection is established by using the method `getConnection` of class `DriverManager`. The method returns an object of class `Connection`. In addition to the resource locator the method requires a login and a password. The following code excerpt shows the connection request.

```
Connection con = DriverManager.getConnection("jdbc:odbc:myDB",
                "myLogin", "myPassword");
```

The connection is established if one of the drivers loaded, and therefore known to the Driver Manager, recognises the specified resource locator. In the example, the connection is established if `myDB` is an ODBC identifier for an available database management system.

At the end of the process, open connections are closed. This is done using the method `close` of class `Connection`.

6.3.3 Manipulation

SQL statements can be executed after the connection is established. It is possible to request the preparation (compilation and optimisation) of an SQL statement by the database management system before its execution. This potentially leads to improved efficiency if the statement is to be executed several times (possibly with different parameters, for instance) since the preparation is factorised for several executions. Such statements are referred to as *prepared SQL statements*. Other statements that are sent to the database management system for both preparation and execution without prior preparation are called *non-prepared SQL statements*.

In both cases, SQL statements are strings passed to the different methods. The string containing the SQL statement can be known at compile time

Section 6.3. Database Connectivity

(static SQL) or constructed at runtime (dynamic SQL). However, the Java^{TM} compiler cannot benefit much from the static nature of an SQL statement since the program will only communicate with the database management system at runtime and only then is it able to request preparation of the statement.

Non-prepared statements are objects of class `Statement` that can be created from an object of class `Connection`. The following code shows that the SQL statement is not provided at creation time since no access plan has to be computed before execution.

```
Connection con;
Statement stmt = con.createStatement();
```

The statement is provided when the statement is executed, by invoking, depending on the statement, the appropriate method of class `Statement`. For a SELECT statement, the method is `executeQuery`. For a DDL and for INSERT, DELETE and UPDATE statements, the method is `executeUpdate`. The following excerpt of code illustrates some of these cases.

```
stmt.executeQuery("SELECT * FROM employee");
stmt.executeUpdate("INSERT INTO employee
                    VALUES ('Stefano Olivaro','Piazzale Roma',
                           'research',1500)");
stmt.executeUpdate("CREATE TABLE task
        (employee_name VARCHAR(24),
         department_name VARCHAR(24),
         start_date DATE,
         end_date DATE,
         task_description VARCHAR(128),
         FOREIGN KEY (employee_name, department_name)
         REFERENCES work_for(employee_name, department_name),
         UNIQUE(employee_name, date)))");
```

Since the preparation of prepared statements is done before execution, the SQL statement has to be specified when the prepared statement, instance of class `PreparedStatement` (sub-class of class `Statement`), is created. The following code illustrates the creation of prepared statements.

```
PreparedStatement query_pstmt =
          con.prepareStatement("SELECT * FROM employee");
PreparedStatement update_pstmt =
          con.prepareStatement("INSERT INTO employee
                                VALUES ('Stefano Olivaro',
                                'Piazzale Roma',
                                'research',1500)");
```

The same methods used for the execution of prepared statements can be used for the execution of non-prepared statements. In this case, however, the SQL statement needs not be specified, as illustrated by the following examples.

```
query_pstmt.executeQuery();
update_pstmt.executeUpdate();
```

It is possible to give a parameterised SQL statement to define a prepared statement. The SQL statement is completed at runtime. Parameters can be identified inside SQL statements by using the symbol ?. For example, the following code creates a prepared statement to find the employees working in a department to be given as a parameter.

```
PreparedStatement query_pstmt =
      con.prepareStatement("SELECT *
                            FROM employee
                            WHERE department = ?");
```

Parameters are identified by their position in the string. Values are assigned to the parameter, before the execution, depending on their type, by using specific **setXXX** methods, where **XXX** denotes the value type. The necessary casting of Java^{TM} types into SQL types is implicitly performed by the Java^{TM} program. For example, Integer Java^{TM} type is converted into INTEGER SQL type, BigDecimal Java^{TM} type into NUMERIC, and String into VARCHAR.

The following example code assigns the value **research** to the parameter of the previous example.

Section 6.3. Database Connectivity

```
query_pstmt.setString(1, 'research');
```

An object of class `ResultSet`, corresponding to the set of t-uples obtained as result, is returned by the execution of a `SELECT` statement. Individual t-uples are accessed using a cursor mechanism implemented as methods of objects of class `ResultSet`.

The cursor initially points before the first t-uple of the result set (and not at the first t-uple). The cursor can then be moved forward using the `next` method. Such method returns `true` if the t-uple exists, `false` otherwise. Different cursor orientations can be specified if the result set has been declared as scrollable. Scrollability can be set when the statement is created. We do neither illustrate nor discuss further this point. Values of the attributes of the fetched t-uple can then be retrieved using the methods `getXXX`, where `XXX` is the Java^{TM} type into which the value to be retrieved has to be cast. Methods `getXXX` take as input either an attribute name or an attribute position. Finally, cursors of the result sets are implicitly closed when the connection is closed. They can also be explicitly closed using the `ResultSet` method `close`.

In the case of null values, extra care must be taken. Indeed, null values are cast by default into a given value for each type, for instance the value 0 for a numeric type. However, for each Java^{TM} base type there exists a built-in class called a *wrapper class*. For example, the wrapper class for `int` is called `Integer`, the wrapper class for `double` is called `Double` etc. The programmer can use objects of these classes and instance variables of these objects to collect the values from the database and deal with null values. We do not illustrate nor discuss this point.

The following code prints the salaries larger than $1000.

```
Statement selstmt = con.createStatement();
String stmt = "SELECT * FROM employee WHERE salary > 1000";
ResultSet  stmt1000 = selstmt.executeQuery (stmt);
while ( stmt1000.next() )
     {
      System.out.println (stmt1000.getString ("salary"));
     }
```

It is possible, using the JDBC^{TM} interface, to create, manipulate and call SQL stored routines. Procedures and functions are created with the appropriate DDL statements as discussed in Section 6.2. In order to call a procedure or a function, the `prepareCall` method of class `Connection` has to be used, obtaining an instance of class `CallableStatement`, which is a subclass of class `PreparedStatement`. A callable statement can then be executed as a prepared statement, by using the method `executeQuery` if the routine body contains a single query, by using the method `executeUpdate` if the routine body contains a single `INSERT/DELETE/UPDATE` or DDL statement, or by using the method `execute` if the routine body contains both updates and queries.

The following example illustrates how the procedure `raise_salary` presented in Section 6.2.3 can be called and executed from a Java^{TM} program using the JDBC^{TM} interface.

```
CallableStatement cs = prepareCall(
              "{call raise_salary('Umberto Lorenzo',500)}");
cs.execute();
```

As opposed to other prepared statements, procedures and function calls may contain both input and output parameters. Input parameters can be assigned by using methods `setXXX`. Output parameters and return values are specified using the method `registerOutParameter` of objects of class `CallableStatement`. For example, consider the function presented in Section 6.2.3. This function has an input parameter and a return value. The following illustrates how the function call can be prepared, how input parameters and return values are managed, and how the obtained result can be retrieved. The Java^{TM} type `BigDecimal` is used to cast the SQL type `NUMERIC`.

```
CallableStatement cs = prepareCall("{? = call avg_salary(?)}");
cs.registerOutParameter(1,Types.NUMERIC);
cs.setString(2,"research");
cs.executeQuery();
BigDecimal n = cs.getBigDecimal(1);
```

6.3.4 Transactions and Exception Handling

By default, the JDBC^{TM} interface transmits every execution to the database as individual transactions. Therefore, every executed statement is ended by default, committed or rolled back by the database system accordingly. This feature called *auto-commit* can be disabled using the method `setAutoCommit` of class `Connection`. The beginning of the execution creates a new transaction. The transaction ends when an explicit `commit` or `rollback` is called or when the execution terminates. After `commit` or `rollback` is called a new transaction begins.

The exceptions raised by the database management system can be caught and handled using the methods of the class `java.sql.SQLException`, which extends the class `java.lang.Exception`. The method `getErrorCode()`, for instance, gets the error code generated by the database management system, and the method `getMessage()` gets an error description. We include examples of usage of these methods in Section 6.3.5.

6.3.5 Example

The following is a complete example of a Java^{TM} program using the JDBC^{TM} interface. The program computes the average salary in the `employee` table and increases the salaries of all employees by 5% if this average salary is less than \$1000. It decreases all the salaries by 5% otherwise. Then it prints the names and salaries of the employees working in a department whose name is given in the variable `my_department`.

A parametric prepared statement is used to pass the name of the department to the SQL statement. For the sake of simplicity, the parameter value corresponds to a specific variable. In a real application such a value could be an input of the application.

```
import java.sql.*;
import java.io.*;

class exampleJDBC
{public static void main (String args [])
  {
```

```
Connection con = null;
try{
    String my_department = "research";
    Class.forName ("sun.jdbc.odbc.JdbcOdbcDriver");
    con =DriverManager.getConnection("jdbc:odbc:my_DB",
                                     "myLogin",
                                     "myPassword");
    con.setAutoCommit(false);
    Statement st = con.createStatement();
    ResultSet rs = st.executeQuery("SELECT AVG(salary)
                                    FROM employee");
    rs.next();
    if (rs.getBigDecimal(1) < 1000)
        st.executeUpdate("UPDATE employee
                          SET salary = salary*1,05");
    else
        st.executeUpdate("UPDATE employee
                          SET salary = salary*0,95");

    PreparedStatement pst =
              con.prepareStatement("SELECT name,salary
                                    FROM employee
                                    WHERE department = ?");
    pst.setString(1,my_department);
    rs = pst.executeQuery();
    while (rs.next())
       System.println("Name: "+rs.getString(1)+
                    "Salary:"+rs.getInt(2));
    con.commit();
    con.close();
    }
    catch(java.lang.ClassNotFoundException e) {
      System.err.print("ClassNotFoundException: ");
      System.err.println(e.getMessage());}
```

Section 6.4. Embedded SQL   97

```
      catch (SQLException e1)
{try{if (con != null) con.rollback();}
      catch (SQLException e) {while( e!=null)
          {
          System.out.println("SQLState: " + e.getSQLState());
          System.out.println("   Code: " + e.getErrorCode());
          System.out.println(" Message: " + e.getMessage());
          e = e.getNextException();
          }}}}}
```

6.4 Embedded SQL

The second solution to external coupling, usually referred to as *embedded SQL*, is the direct embedding of SQL statements inside an extension of a programming language. The resulting language supports all computational functionalities of the original language and uses SQL to directly access and manipulate data. In a program, SQL statements can appear anywhere any statement of the host language appears.

In the following, we introduce the reference architecture for embedded SQL. Then, we describe how connection, manipulation, transaction and exception handling can be programmed.

6.4.1 Reference Architecture

In order to distinguish SQL statements from commands of the host language, any SQL statement must be clearly identified by using some prefix and terminator. In many embedded SQL extensions of C, Pascal, Fortran and COBOL the prefix is the keyword **EXEC SQL**. According to SQLj, an ANSI/ISO standard specifications for ways to use the Java^{TM} programming language with, the prefix is #sql and the terminator is the semicolon.

Before compiling the program, a preprocessor transforms the embedded SQL program written in an extension of a language L into a program in the pure language L in which the proper connection to the database management system has been added using a database connectivity solution, and the embedded SQL statements have been translated into calls to the database management systems using the corresponding CLI. The resulting program can be compiled with the standard compiler of language L.

Even if successive versions of the SQL standard specify how SQL is best embedded into a programming language, the detailed syntax may depend on the host language, database management system, as well as on choices by the designer of the solution.

In the following, we discuss embedded SQL using SQLj and an Oracle $9i^{TM}$ database. The preprocessor of SQLj is part of a *translator*. The translator reads an SQLj source file, with extension `*.sqlj`, containing embedded SQL statements and translates it into a $Java^{TM}$ source file, with extension `*.java`, containing calls to the available SQLj runtime libraries (possibly using the $JDBC^{TM}$ interface, for instance), depending on the chosen database management system. The translator also generates a profile file for each connection required by the application. The file contains information about the SQL statements to be executed in the context of each connection. The SQLj translator finally compiles the $Java^{TM}$ source file into byte codes.

6.4.2 Connection

The connection with the database management system is established by calling the method `connect` defined in the class corresponding to the particular database management system. Similarly to the $JDBC^{TM}$ `getConnection` method, the `connect()` method accepts three parameters: a resource locator in the $JDBC^{TM}$ syntax, a username and a password. The following example illustrates the connection to an Oracle $9i^{TM}$ database in SQLj assuming a driver of type 1.

`oracle.connect("jdbc:odbc:my_DB","myLogin","myPassword");`

At the end of the process, an open connection must be closed, by using method `close`.

6.4.3 Manipulation

SQL statements in SQLj can only be static statements.

Section 6.4. Embedded SQL

SQL statements are preceded by the keyword **#sql**, terminated by a semicolon and placed inside curly brackets, as illustrated below.

```
#sql {SQL_statement};
```

For example, the following SQLj statement inserts a new employee in the database.

```
#sql {INSERT INTO employee VALUES ('Stefano Olivaro',
                                   'Piazzale Roma',
                                   'research',1500)};
```

Java^{TM} variables can be used inside SQL statement to represent values. They must be preceded by a colon in order to distinguish them from table attributes. The type compatibility between the host language and SQL is part of the embedded SQL definition. An implicit casting is performed each time a variable is used inside an SQL statement. The casting rules are similar for SQLj and the JDBC^{TM} interface.

For each host variable used inside an SQL statement, a mode can be optionally specified in order to describe how the SQL statement is going to use such value. The keyword **IN** is used if the SQL statement reads the value of the variable. The keyword **OUT** is used if the SQL statement changes the value of the variable. The keyword **INOUT** is used if the SQL statement both reads and writes the value of the variable.

In a similar way, the SQL statements can include references to other Java^{TM} elements such as array elements, object attributes and function calls.

The result of the evaluation of a **SELECT** statement returning a single row can be collected into some Java^{TM} variables (one for each attribute value) using the **SELECT INTO** statement as illustrated in the following example.

```
String department = 'research';
BigDecimal my_budget;
#sql{SELECT budget INTO :my_budget
     FROM department
     WHERE name = :department};
```

The default mode for a variable in an **INTO** clause is **OUT**. The default mode for a variable in a **WHERE** clause is **IN**. **IN** variables can also be used in the SET and WHERE parts of an UPDATE statement, in the WHERE part of a DELETE statement and in the VALUES part of an INSERT statement.

If the query returns more than one t-uple, a cursor must be used to process the results. In SQLj, a cursor is an instance of an *iterator* class. An iterator class must be defined by the application for each result type to be analysed. An iterator class contains an attribute declaration for each attribute of the t-uples to be processed. The definition of an iterator class has the following form.

```
#sql iterator iterator_name (attribute_declaration);
```

For example, the following statement defines an iterator class for t-uples with the two attributes name and salary.

```
#sql iterator EmpIter (String name, Real salary);
```

The result of the evaluation of a SELECT statement is assigned to an instance of the iterator class. The next() method moves the cursor to the next t-uple in the result set. If such a t-uple exists the method evaluates to true, otherwise it evaluates to false. Different cursor orientations can be specified if the iterator has been declared as scrollable. Scrollability can be set when the iterator is defined. We do neither illustrate nor discuss further this point. Iterator objects support one accessor method for each attribute. Accessor methods can be used to retrieve values of the fetched t-uple. An iterator can finally be closed by using method close. The following example illustrates this mechanism by using the iterator class EmpIter, defined previously.

```
EmpIter my_empiter = null;
#sql my_empiter = {SELECT name, salary FROM employee};
while (my_empiter.next()) {
   System.out.println("Name: " + my_empiter.name());
   System.out.println("Salary: " + my_empiter.salary());}
my_empiter.close();
```

It is possible, in SQLj, to create, manipulate and call SQL stored routines. Procedures and functions are created with the appropriate DDL statements as discussed in Section 6.2.

Section 6.4. Embedded SQL

Procedures calls have the following form.

```
#sql {CALL procedure_call};
```

Functions evaluations have the following form.

```
#sql host_variable = {VALUES function_call};
```

6.4.4 Transactions and Exception Handling

By default, SQLj requires explicit `COMMIT` and `ROLLBACK` statements in the following syntax, respectively.

```
#sql {COMMIT};
#sql {ROLLBACK};
```

Auto-commit of each DML statement can be specified when connecting to the database. For example, in the Oracle 9i^{TM} database management system, an additional Boolean parameter for the `connect` method can be given. If the parameter is true auto-commit is enabled, otherwise it is disabled. The following example illustrates how auto-commit can be enabled.

```
oracle.connect("jdbc:odbc:my_DB","myLogin","myPassword",true);
```

The catching and handling of exceptions is similar to the mechanism presented in Section 6.3.4 for the JDBC^{TM} interface.

6.4.5 Example

The following is a complete example of a Java^{TM} program using SQLj. The program computes the average salary in the `employee` table and increases the salaries of all employees by 5% if the average salary is less than $1000. It decreases all the salaries by 5% otherwise. Then it prints the names and salaries of the employees working in a department whose name is given in the variable `my_department`.

A variable is used to specify the name of the department in the last SQL statement. In a real application such a value could be an input of the application.

```
import java.sql.*;
import java.io.*;
import java.math.*;
import sqlj.runtime.*;
import sqlj.runtime.ref.*;
import oracle.sqlj.runtime.*;
import java.sql.*;

class exampleSQLj
{
 #sql iterator Name_Salary_Iter(String name, int salary);

 public static void main (String args [])
 {
 try{
     BigDecimal avg_sal;
     String my_department = "research";
     oracle.connect("jdbc:odbc:my_DB",
                    "myLogin",
                    "myPassword",
                    false);
     #sql{SELECT AVG(salary) INTO :avg_sal FROM employee};
     if (avg_sal > 1000)
         #sql{UPDATE employee SET salary = salary*1,05};
     else
         #sql{UPDATE employee SET salary = salary*0,95};

     Name_Salary_Iter my_iter = null;
     #sql my_iter ={SELECT name,salary
                    FROM employee
                    WHERE department = :my_department};
     while (my_iter.next())
        System.println("Name: "+my_iter.name()+
                       "Salary:"+my_iter.salary())
```

Section 6.4. Embedded SQL

```
    #sql{COMMIT};
}
catch(java.lang.ClassNotFoundException e) {
  System.err.print("ClassNotFoundException: ");
  System.err.println(e.getMessage());}
catch (SQLException e1) {
  try{if (con != null) con.rollback();}
catch (SQLException e) {
  while( e!=null){
    System.out.println("SQLState: " + e.getSQLState());
    System.out.println("   Code: " + e.getErrorCode());

    System.out.println(" Message: " + e.getMessage());
    e = e.getNextException();}}}}}
```

Chapter 7

Entity-Relationship Model

7.1 Entities and Relationships

The entity-relationship (ER) model is a conceptual data model. Peter Chen first presented it in 1975 in the seminal article "The Entity-Relationship Model: Toward a Unified View of Data" (see Stonebraker and Hellerstein, 1998).

The designer modelling an application using the entity-relationship model should not worry about the logical model. This is of course true to the extent of the assumptions that are embedded in the entity-relationship model constructs and to the extent of the limited choices the model offers. By definition, a model is a restricted set of constructs. The entity-relationship model relies on the claim that describing sets of homogeneous entities and sets of generic relationships among these entities is sufficiently conceptually rich. Entities and relationships belong to a named set. Entities in an entity set have the same attributes. Relationships in a relationship set have the same roles and attributes. Similarly to the relational model being a value-based logical data model, the entity-relationship model is a value-based conceptual model. Entities can be distinguished within an entity set thanks to the values of their attributes only. Relationships can be distinguished within a relationship set by the entities they link only. This is the fundamental difference with object-oriented models. As a consequence, an entity set with no attribute can have at most one entity.

Entities are meant to represent entities and objects of the real world relevant to the application. How concrete and tangible these real world entities are depend on the designer and little can be argued scientifically about this point. Relationships are meant to represent real world associations, which are relevant to the application, among the real world entities identified. Again the nature and choice of associations to be represented and the details of their representation are often a subjective matter. It is possible to find dual conceptual modelling choices in which entities are relationships and vice versa.

One of the great tools coming with the entity-relationship model is the entity-relationship diagram. The entity-relationship diagram is a graphical representation of entity sets and relationship sets. The diagram is a good visual support for the design of reasonably complex database applications.

Entities in the entity-relationship model are similar to t-uples in the relational model. Entities are elements of a Cartesian product of domains. Each participating domain in the Cartesian product is associated with a named attribute. We consider scalar values only, although it is not uncommon to see variants of the entity-relationship model that accept complex domains for the attributes of entities. Such variants can usually be mapped to a model with scalar attributes. The designer defines sets of entities of the same kind, i.e., entities representing the same real world concept and having the same attributes. Entity sets in the entity-relationship model are therefore similar to relations in the relational model. Entity sets are homogeneous collections of structured data. Figure 7.1 illustrates the graphical representation of an entity set. A box labelled with the name of the set represents the entity set.

Entity Set Name

Figure 7.1: Entity Set

The attributes of the entities in the entity sets are drawn as lines leaving the box and ending with a small circle as illustrated in Figure 7.2. The lines are labelled with the name of the attribute. The domain of the attribute should also be indicated in the label of a line. Usual domains are strings, real numbers, Booleans or dates. We prefer, however, to consider a single scalar domain (union of all the above) and delay the choice of a more specific domain to the next stage of the design: the mapping to the logical model. It is therefore not necessary in the rest of this chapter to indicate the domain next to the attribute name.

Individual entities are fully identified by a unique combination of the

Section 7.1. Entities and Relationships

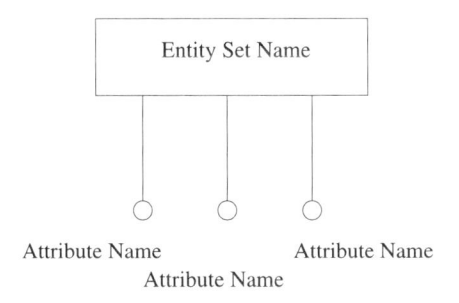

Figure 7.2: Attributes of Entity Sets

values of their attributes. There cannot be two entities with the same values for all their attributes. Two such entities would be the same entity.

Relationships are elements of a Cartesian product of entity sets and domains. Entity sets contribute to roles of the relationships, while domains contribute to attributes of the relationships. The designer defines sets of relationships of the same kind, i.e., relationships representing the same real world concept and having the same roles and attributes. A relationship set is represented by a lozenge labelled with the name of the set as illustrated in Figure 7.3.

Figure 7.3: Relationship Set

Attributes of relationships are drawn similarly to attributes of entities. Figure 7.4 shows the representation of attributes of a relationship.

The entity sets involved in the relationship set are linked to the lozenge representing the relationship set. Figure 7.5 illustrates the representation of a relationship set linking two entity sets. The roles of the entity sets involved in a relationship can be named. This is illustrated by Figure 7.6.

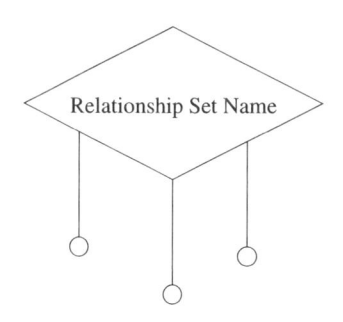

Figure 7.4: Attributes of Relationship Sets

Figure 7.5: Entity and Relationship Sets

Although binary relationships are most common, relationships may be of any arity. Figure 7.7 illustrates the representation of a ternary relationship. Notice that there can be unary relationships. We encourage the reader to think about examples of real world concepts that could be represented with unary, tertiary or higher arity relationships.

Figure 7.8 is an entity-relationship diagram for the conceptual modelling of a database application involving employees and departments of a company. The employees have a first and last name, an address and a salary. The departments have a name and a location. The employees work for a department. They have been hired at a given date.

An entity set may play several roles in a relationship set. Figure 7.9 illustrates an example of such a situation. Relationships in the relationship set `married`, with roles `husband` and `wife`, link two entities from the entity set `person`. This is not to be confused with the unary relationships mentioned above.

Relationships are fully identified by the entities involved. For instance,

Section 7.1. Entities and Relationships

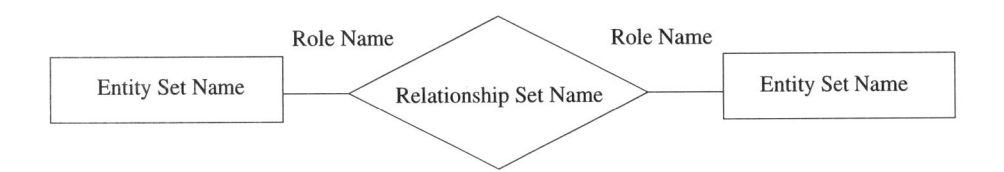

Figure 7.6: Named Roles

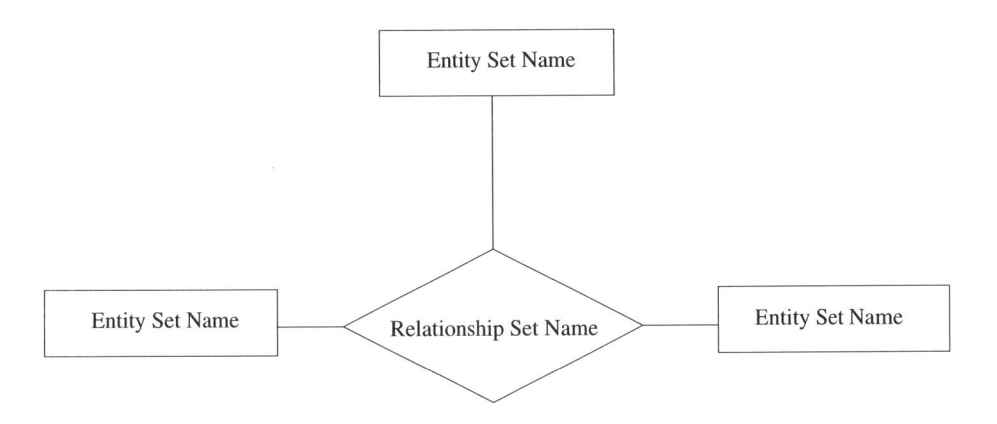

Figure 7.7: Ternary Relationship Set

according to the entity-relationship diagram of Figure 7.8, it is possible to have an employee working for several departments. Conversely, a department can have several employees working for it. It is neither compulsory for employees to work nor for departments to have employees. The attributes of a relationship do not participate to its identity. The entity-relationship diagram of Figure 7.8 forbids the case of an employee working for a department on several contracts with different hiring dates. If such a representation is intended, the designer needs to modify the entity-relationship diagram, probably by adding an entity set reifying the concept of contract and changing the binary `work_for` relationship set into a ternary one with a new role linking it to the `contract` entity sets.

110   *Chapter 7. Entity-Relationship Model*

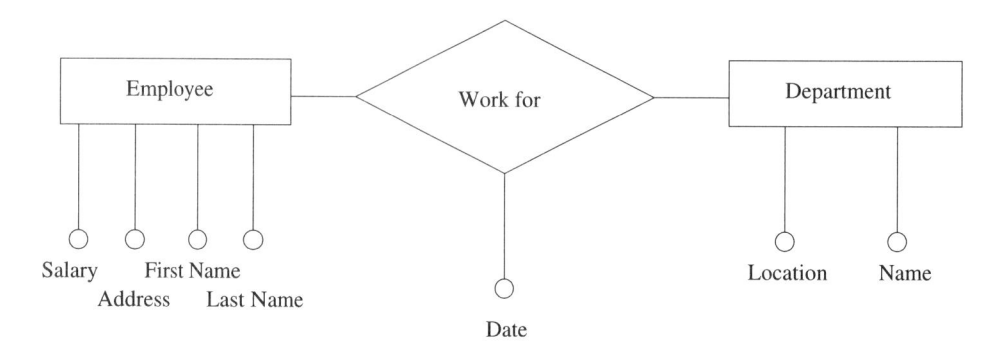

Figure 7.8: Entity and Relationship Sets

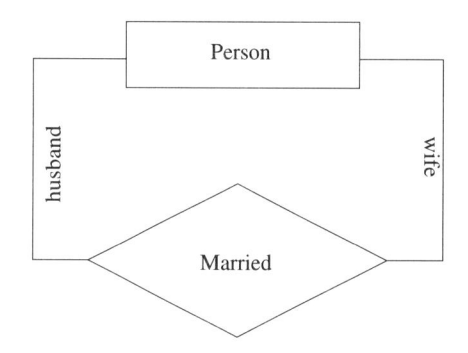

Figure 7.9: Reflexive Relationship Sets

7.2 Constraints

7.2.1 Implicit and Explicit Constraints

The modelling of a database application in terms of entity sets and relationship sets has already implicitly captured a number of constraints. For instance, it is not possible to have two entities in the same entity set with the same values for their attributes, and there can be only one relationship between any two entities, regardless of the possible values of the relationship's attributes. Such constraints are structural.

The entity-relationship model also allows the explicit expression of con-

Section 7.2. Constraints

straints. The additional constraints that can be expressed are *key constraints*, defining the identity of entities, and *participation constraints*, limiting the cardinality of the participation of entities from an entity set to relationships of a relationship set.

Extensions and variants of the basic entity-relationship model allow additional constraints. They also may use variant notations to express the constraints and constructs presented in this section. The reader is encouraged to compare the notations in this book with those in the textbooks mentioned in Chapter 9, and to try and translate the examples here and there from one to the other notation. The notations that we use here are not the most conventional. However, they have the clear advantage, we believe, to be explicit.

7.2.2 Identity

It is very often the case that one or a subset of the attributes of an entity be sufficient to fully identify the entities in an identity set. Such an attribute and such a set of attributes are called a *key*.

Keys composed of a single attribute are represented by black circles on the representation of this attribute, as shown in Figure 7.10, while keys composed of several attributes are represented by black circles on participating attributes linked by a line ended by a black circle, as shown in Figure 7.11. We call the latter *composite keys*.

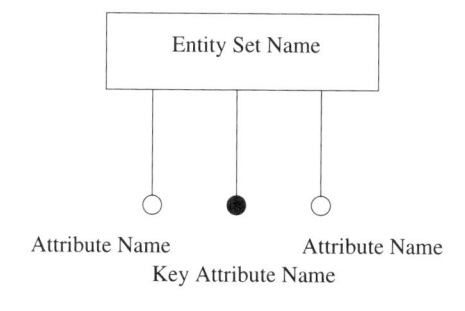

```
          ┌──────────────────┐
          │  Entity Set Name │
          └────┬────┬────┬───┘
               │    │    │
               ○    ●    ○
     Attribute Name    Attribute Name
               Key Attribute Name
```

Figure 7.10: Key

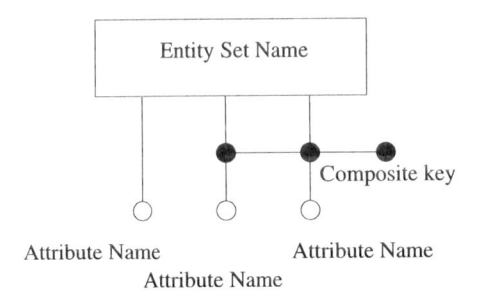

Figure 7.11: Composite Key

In the example in the previous section, we can refine our modelling by indicating that the first name and last name of an employee together are sufficient to identify the employee, and that the name of a department alone is sufficient to identify the department as illustrated in Figure 7.12. This must agree with the logic of the application. Indeed, such a conceptual design assumes that there are not and will not be homonyms in the company, and that there are not and will not be departments with the same name at different locations.

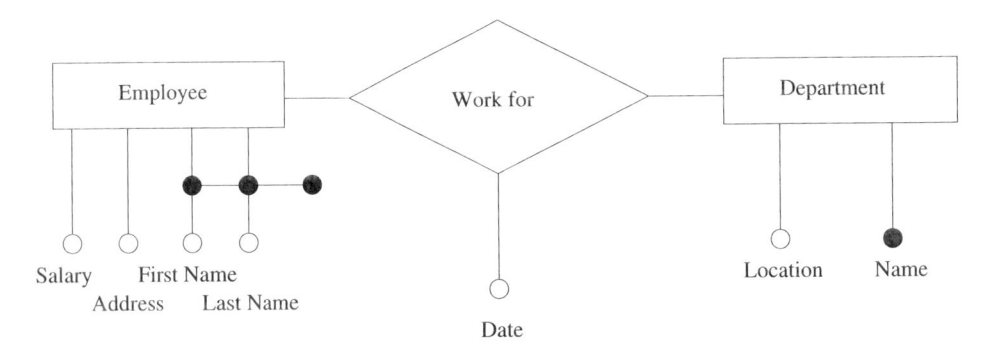

Figure 7.12: Entity and Relationship Sets

It is of course possible to identify several possible keys. At this conceptual design phase we favour the option that notes all these keys on the ER diagram. This is made possible by the unambiguous notation we use for

Section 7.2. Constraints 113

single-attribute-keys and composite keys (notice the ambiguity of most other authors' notations). However, for the sake of simplicity and to comply with most authors, we suggest choosing among the candidates and representing one key only for each entity set.

7.2.3 Participation

Each entity in an entity sets involved with a relationship set may or may not be participating in a relationship. Furthermore, if it participates, it may participate in more than one relationship. On each line linking an entity set to a relationship set we may indicate the minimum cardinality x and the maximum cardinality y of the participation in the form of a couple (x, y). The values of x and y can be 0, 1 or any integer, or N or M to indicate an unconstrained value. N and M are symbols representing unconstraint values but they neither represent any value in particular nor are they variables. It is therefore possible to have several occurrences of N or M on a diagram that represents different maximum cardinalities. Figure 7.13 shows how the participation constraints are represented on the entity-relationship diagrams.

Figure 7.13: Participation Constraints

Certain patterns of participation constraints have been given canonical names (notice that, in the definitions below, x represents some value; it is different from N or M, which represents unconstrained cardinality):

- a participation constraint of the form (1, x) is called a *mandatory* or *total* participation;

- a participation constraint of the form (0, x) is called an *optional* or *partial* participation;

- a participation constraint of the form (x, 1) for all entity sets involved characterises a *one-to-one* relationship;

- a participation constraint of the form (x, 1) for one entity set involved and of (x, y) for the others, where y = N, M or any integer bigger than 1, characterises a *one-to-many* relationship;

- a participation constraint of the form (x, y) for all entity sets involved, where y = N, M or any integer bigger than 1, characterises a *many-to-many* relationship.

The example represented in Figure 7.14 illustrates a set, manage, of one-to-one relationships between entities of the entity sets department and employee. The participation of entities in the entity set department is mandatory or total. The participation of entities in the entity set employee is optional or partial.

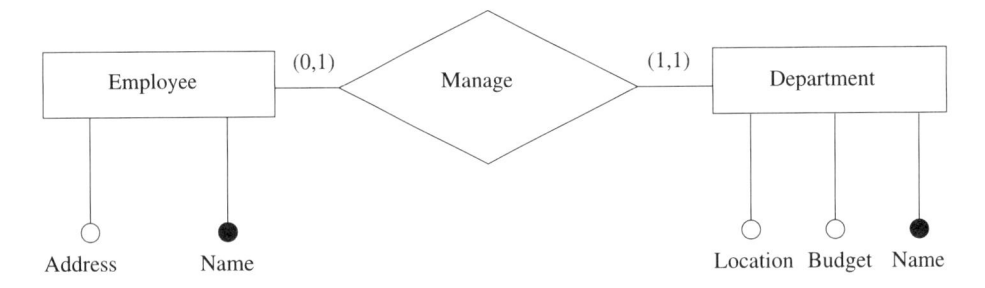

Figure 7.14: Participation Constraints

Figure 7.15 is a complete entity-relationship diagram for the example we have introduced and used in Chapters 2 and 5.

7.2.4 Weak Entities

There is an exception to the general rule according to which entities are identified by the values of their attributes. This special case is the case of a weak entity set. Weak entities are identified in the scope of other entities to which they are associated in a relationship and that we call dominant

Section 7.2. Constraints   115

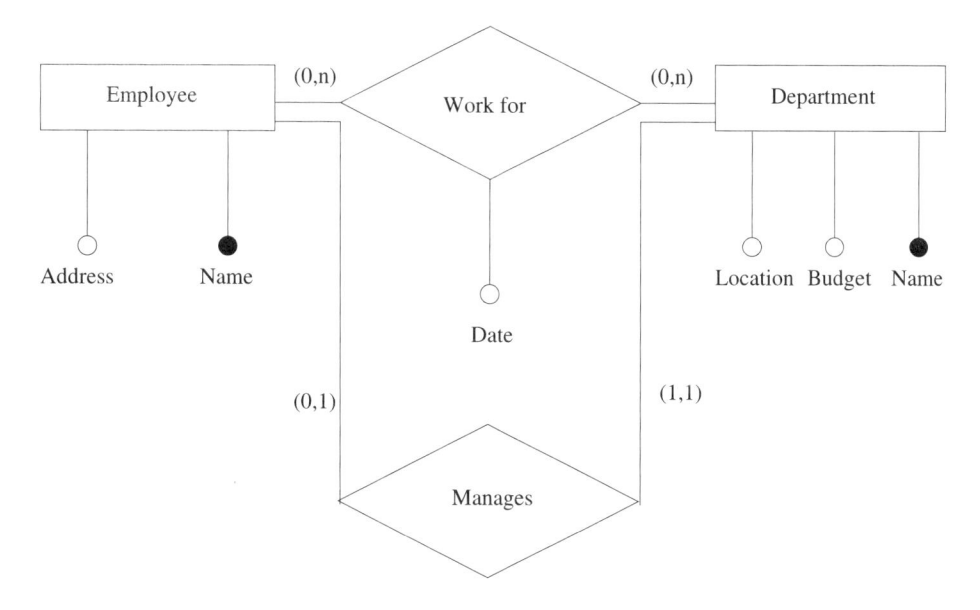

Figure 7.15: Entity-Relationship Diagram of the Running Example

entities. There can be more than one dominant entity if the weak entity is involved in a relationship of arity greater than 2. As illustrated in Figure 7.16, the attributes of the (weak) key of the weak entity are linked to the entity set (or sets if there are several dominant entities for a single weak entity) under which the identity is defined. A key for a weak entity is composed of the identifying attributes of the weak entity, or internal key attributes, together with the key attributes of the dominant entities, or external key attributes. The notation that we use is more flexible than that of many other authors. It allows unambiguous specification of several possible keys of an entity (including a mixture of weak and non-weak keys) as well as a selection of some dominant entities in the case of higher arity relationships.

Since the identity of a weak entity is determined in the scope of dominant entities with which it is associated in a relationship it is natural to constrain the participation of the weak entity to the relationship. Indeed, every weak entity needs to be involved in at least one relationship so that a dominant

116   Chapter 7. Entity-Relationship Model

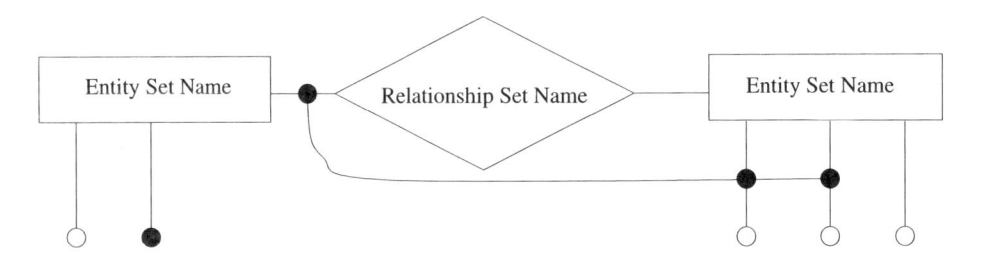

Figure 7.16: Weak Entity Set

entity exists. The minimum participation cardinality is 1. Every weak entity can be involved in at most one relationship of the relationship set that defines the weak entity since the identification must be unique. The maximum participation cardinality is 1. Therefore, the participation constraint is expressed as (1, 1). These statements require further explanation. Indeed, it may not be clear what we mean by 'the weak entity' and its 'participation'. These terms refer to the entity as identified by its internal key attributes and by the external key attributes of the dominant entity. If we ignore the weak entity identification, the participation constraint would be (1, N), mandatory in a many-to-many-relationship. Figure 7.17 shows explicitly the participation constraint for a weak entity as conventionally indicated (i.e., (1, 1)).

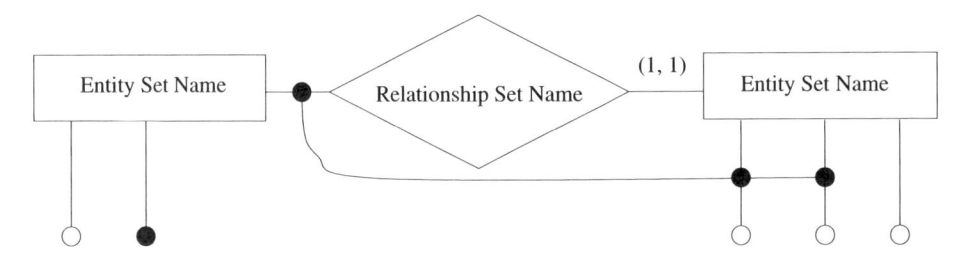

Figure 7.17: Participation Cardinality of a Weak Entity Set

Figure 7.18 shows an example of a weak entity. Students are registered at universities. Yet, the universities independently give out matric numbers, which identify the students. Therefore, the correct identification of a student

Section 7.3. Mapping ER Diagrams to Relational Schemas   117

is the pair of attributes `matric`, its internal key attribute, and `name` (of the university), its external attribute. The entity set `university` is the dominant entity of the weak entity set `student` under the relationship set `registered`. We write that the participation constraint is (1,1); there can be two students named Arnold Wijaya with matric number `1234X13`, for example, provided one is registered at the National University of Singapore and the other one at Nanyang Technological University, two universities in the `university` entity set.

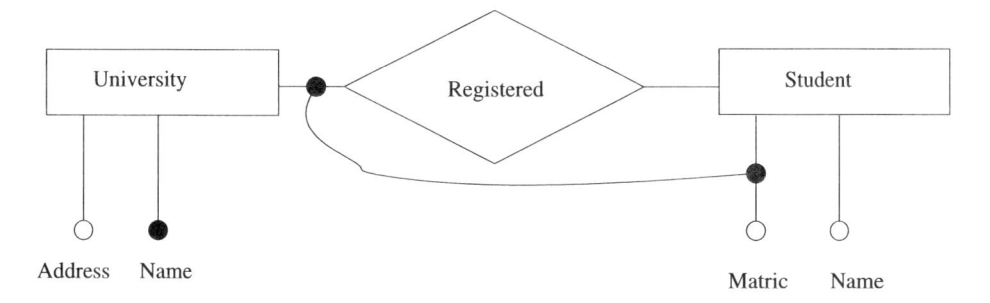

Figure 7.18: Weak Entity Set

Notice that, unlike suggested by the very term 'weak entity', this property is not necessarily intrinsic to the entity but rather to its identification. Indeed, one could imagine an entity set whose members can be identified by either a combination of their attributes or a combination of their attributes under a dominant entity. In the example of Figure 7.18, we could add an attribute to represent the passport or national identification number of the students. This attribute alone would constitute an alternate key. We should therefore talk about *weak identification* or *weak key* rather than weak entities.

7.3 Mapping ER Diagrams to Relational Schemas

Once the conceptual design is complete, the next task is to translate it into a logical design. This phase is a translation of the entity-relationship diagram into a set of definitions for relations, integrity constraints and possibly views (we do not show examples of the latter here). In general, several choices are left to the designer in this phase of the design of the database application. Several of these choices are related to the tuning of performance. They require that the designer takes into account the database management system and workload (typical queries and interactions with the database). In the absence of specific information about the database management system and the workload, ignoring general performance issues, the designer can proceed to a translation with the sole objective of preserving the semantics captured in the conceptual design, as much as possible.

The main task of the designer is therefore to choose a logical schema that, not only allows the representation of entities and relationships in the entity-relationship model, but also enforces as many as possible of the constraints, structural, key, referential and participation constraints, that have been captured. Ultimately, some constraints may not be enforced. This may be the case when the constraints can only be expressed using check constraints or assertions which the database management system targeted does not support. A typical example of a constraint that may be ignored in the translation is a participation constraint of the form (0, 5) for the enforcement of the upper bound of which an SQL constraint involving a COUNT aggregate function is required.

In this section, we present the patterns of translation from the entity-relationship diagram to a relational schema. We illustrate these patterns with examples. Most of the time these examples are similar but slightly different ones are also used at times.

Let us start with the entity-relationship diagram in Figure 7.19. Entity sets are translated into relations. Concretely, they become tables. The attributes of the corresponding tables are the attributes of the entity set and their domains are the domains, available in the SQL dialect of the database management system, that best match the domains in the conceptual design. Since we have purposely ignored domains in the entity-relationship diagrams, we choose the domains for the attributes of the relations. The attributes composing a key of the entity set are declared to form a primary key of the table.

The entity set department, in Figure 7.19, is translated into the table department. We give the following SQL definition of the table.

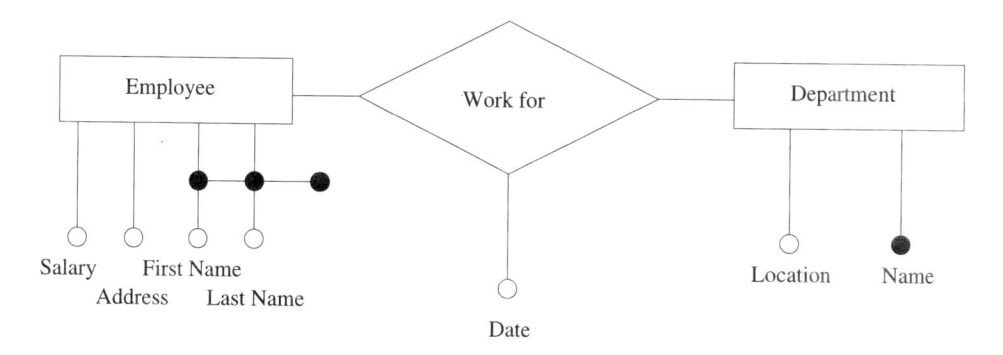

Section 7.3. Mapping ER Diagrams to Relational Schemas

Figure 7.19: Entity and Relationship Sets

```
CREATE TABLE department
  (name VARCHAR(24) PRIMARY KEY,
   location VARCHAR(36));
```

Similarly, the entity set employee, in Figure 7.19, is translated into the table employee. We give below the SQL definition of the table.

```
CREATE TABLE employee
  (first_name VARCHAR(24),
   last_name VARCHAR(24),
   address VARCHAR(36),
   salary NUMERIC,
   PRIMARY KEY (first_name, last_name));
```

Relationship sets are also translated into relations. Yet, the attributes of the relations are not only the attributes of the relationship itself, but also the key attributes of all the participating entity sets. Indeed, the composite key, made up by the keys of the participating entities, identifies a relationship in the set. The relationship set work_for, in Figure 7.19, is translated into the table work_for. Below is the SQL definition of the table.

```
CREATE TABLE work_for
  (first_name VARCHAR(24),
   last_name VARCHAR(24),
```

```
  name VARCHAR(24),
  date DATE,
  PRIMARY KEY (first_name, last_name, name),
  FOREIGN KEY (first_name, last_name)
          REFERENCES employee(first_name, last_name),
  FOREIGN KEY (name) REFERENCES department(name));
```

The key of the table is indeed composed of the key attributes of both the **employee** and the **department** tables. Furthermore, since a `work_for` relationship only exists between entities from the entity sets **employee** and **department** and in order to guarantee the referential integrity, foreign key constraints are declared. They require that the values for the attributes `first_name` and `last_name`, and `name` exist in the tables **employee** and **department**, respectively.

General cardinality constraints must be expressed with generalised dependencies. Concretely, they are translated in SQL into `UNIQUE` or generalised constraints involving the `COUNT()` aggregate function. However, in some cases, they can be translated into structural constraints by an appropriate choice of the logical schema. For instance, the constraint on the cardinality of the participation of an entity set to a one-to-many relationship can be enforced in the translation by using the key of this one entity set as the only key of the relationship. In the example in Figure 7.14, since one employee at most manages a department, the department name can be a key of the relationship **manage**. In other words, the maximum cardinality constraint of 1 for the participation of entities of the entity set **department** in relationships of the relationship set **manage** can be enforced by the following translation of the relationship set into the table **manage**.

```
CREATE TABLE manage
  (manager_name VARCHAR(24) UNIQUE,
   department_name VARCHAR(24),
   PRIMARY KEY (department_name),
   FOREIGN KEY (manager_name) REFERENCES employee(name),
   FOREIGN KEY (department_name) REFERENCES department(name));
```

This ensures that a department has at most one manager.

Section 7.3. Mapping ER Diagrams to Relational Schemas

The entity set `employee` has also a maximum cardinality of 1. Indeed, conversely, a manager is in charge of at most one department. This is enforced in this example by the `UNIQUE` constraint. Yet, we could alternatively choose the name of the manager as the key. Therefore, we could translate the relationship set as follows.

```
CREATE TABLE manage
  (manager_name VARCHAR(24),
   department_name VARCHAR(24) UNIQUE,
   PRIMARY KEY (manager_name),
   FOREIGN KEY (manager_name) REFERENCES employee(name),
   FOREIGN KEY (department_name) REFERENCES department(name));
```

For the enforcement of both upper bounds of the participation constraints of employees and department we can use `UNIQUE` constraints and normally declare the primary key (`manager_name`, `department_name`).

Furthermore, the mandatory participation of entities of an entity set in a one-to-many relationship can be translated into a table combining both the tables resulting from the translation of the entity set and of the relationship set. In summary, in the example in Figure 7.14, in order to enforce all cardinality constraints, we combine the two tables resulting from the translation of the entity set `department` and of the relationship set `manage` into a single table, that we call `department_manage`, and which is defined as follows.

```
CREATE TABLE department_manage
  (manager_name VARCHAR(24) UNIQUE,
   department_name VARCHAR(24),
   location VARCHAR(36),
   budget NUMERIC,
   PRIMARY KEY (department_name),
   FOREIGN KEY (manager_name) REFERENCES employee(name));
```

A similar situation occurs for weak entities. We need only remember that the mandatory, one-to-many relationship represented assumes that the weak entity is identified with a combination of its internal keys and the keys of the dominant entity. Let us consider the translation of the weak entity set `student` in the example illustrated in Figure 7.18. We can combine the two tables resulting from the translation of the weak entity set and the relationship set into a single table, call it `student_registered`, and define it as follows.

```
CREATE TABLE student_registered
  (matric VARCHAR(12),
   university_name VARCHAR(24),
   student_name VARCHAR(24),
   PRIMARY KEY (matric, university_name),
   FOREIGN KEY (university_name) REFERENCES university(name));
```

The key of this table is the key of the relationship, i.e., the key of the dominant entity combined with the locally identifying attributes of the weak entity, in the examples: `university_name` and `matric`, respectively.

It seems that we have now completed the logical design of our database application. We have written the SQL DML statements to create the tables with the necessary integrity constraints in the relational database management system that we are using. We could, at this stage proceed to programming the rest of the application, in particular the update and query procedures. However, additional refinements of the logical design may be needed; we will discuss them in Chapter 8.

Chapter 8

Normalisation

8.1 Anomalies and Decomposition

8.1.1 Anomalies

After the translation of the Entity-Relationship diagram into a relational schema following the rules we have proposed in Chapter 7, the logical design of a database application involves two additional tasks: namely normalisation and tuning. Tuning generally aims at improving the efficiency of the application. Tuning is the modification of the logical design according to physical characteristics of the data, workload, hardware and software (database management system). Normalisation generally aims at improving the effectiveness of the design and at avoiding anomalies in the representation of the application data. Normalisation is the modification of the design according to semantic characteristics of the data such as functional dependencies and other integrity constraints. In practice, tuning and normalisation often overlap or conflict.

In this chapter, we present and discuss the most common forms of normalisation, i.e., the decomposition into Boyce-Codd and third normal forms using functional dependencies.

First, we illustrate with examples the possible anomalies. Then we study functional dependencies and their properties. Armed with these tools, we look at the definition of two normal forms that protect us from the above-mentioned anomalies and at the corresponding normalisation algorithms that help us remove the anomalies while preserving the semantics of the design. Finally, we briefly mention more advanced normal forms.

Let us consider a schema containing a relation *employee* with the following scheme, which is used to store the names of employees together with their addresses, the positions they hold in the company and their salaries:

employee(*name, address, position, salary*).

Let us assume that the company imposes a rule that salaries be fixed for a given position. We can observe in Figure 8.1 that the design choices that led to the above scheme for the relation *employee*, given the business rule expressed, create several potential problems. Such problems are called *design anomalies* or, simply, anomalies. Four kinds of anomalies are illustrated by our example instance in Figure 8.1.

name	address	department	position	salary
Dewi Srijaya	12a Jln Lempeng	Toys	Clerk	2000
Izabel Leong	10 Outram Park	Sports	Trainee	1200
John Smith	107 Clementi Rd	Toys	Clerk	2000
Axel Bayer	55 Cuscaden Rd	Sports	Trainee	1200
Winny Lee	10 West Coast Rd	Sports	Manager	2500
Sylvia Tok	22 East Coast Lane	Toys	Manager	2600
Eric Wei	100 Jurong Drive	Toys	Assistant	2200
			Security Guard	1500

Figure 8.1: Anomalies

The first kind of anomaly is a redundant usage of the storage. In the example instance in Figure 8.1, the salary of a clerk is stored twice. This is unnecessary since all clerks are supposed to have the same salary according to the business rule. Therefore, it appears that the storage of the salary together with each individual is redundant. Such an anomaly is naturally called a *redundant storage anomaly*.

Data entry errors may occur when storing the salary of a certain category of personnel several times. It is the case with the salary of managers. In the example instance in Figure 8.1, we see two managers with different salaries. Such a situation should not have occurred and should be prevented. Such an anomaly is called an *update anomaly* since it can be caused by an erroneous update of a value of an attribute governed by the business rule.

Let us assume that we delete the record of Eric Wei in the example instance in Figure 8.1. This record is the only record of an assistant currently stored in the database. After deletion we have lost the information about

Section 8.1. Anomalies and Decomposition   125

the salary of assistants. Here again, the embedment of the information about salaries and positions into the table *employee* leads us to a possible anomaly called a *deletion anomaly* since it may occur after deletion of a t-uple. Conversely, should we want to keep this knowledge, or as it is illustrated in the example instance in Figure 8.1, the knowledge that a security guard earns $1500, we need to either insert a personal record for that purpose or make use of null values. This anomaly is called an *insertion anomaly*.

8.1.2 Lossless Decomposition

Anomalies occur because of a design conflicting with some integrity constraints. Indeed, the business rule that we have given is a functional dependency declaring that the position determines the salary. Therefore, the relation *employee* contains information about two related but different entities: employees, with their names, addresses and positions, and the position with its salary. This situation can be avoided by decomposing the relation *employee* into two relations with the following schemes:

$$employee1(name, address, position)$$

and

$$position(position, salary).$$

This decomposition is illustrated in Figure 8.2.

The decomposition of a relation scheme leads to a set of relation schemes, i.e., several relations whose attributes are attributes of the original relation. All attributes of the original relation must at least appear in one of the new relations.

Definition 8.1 *A set S of relation schemes is a decomposition of a relation scheme R if and only if*

- $\forall R_i \in S, R_i \subset R$ and
- $R \subset \bigcup_{R_i \in S} R_i$.

name	address	department	position
Dewi Srijaya	12a Jln Lempeng	Toys	Clerk
Izabel Leong	10 Outram Park	Sports	Trainee
John Smith	107 Clementi Rd	Toys	Clerk
Axel Bayer	55 Cuscaden Rd	Sports	Trainee
Winny Lee	10 West Coast Rd	Sports	Manager
Sylvia Tok	22 East Coast Lane	Toys	Manager
Eric Wei	100 Jurong Drive	Toys	Assistant

position	salary
Clerk	2000
Trainee	1200
Manager	2500
Assistant	2200
Security Guard	1500

Figure 8.2: Decomposition

We call the schemes in the decomposition *fragments*. Notice that the fragments are not necessarily disjoint. On the contrary, some should overlap so that the original relation can be recovered by joining the fragments on the overlapping attributes. We must indeed make sure that the decomposition is *lossless*, i.e., the decomposition must be able to maintain the data the original relation could represent under the integrity constraints. The decomposed schema may be able to represent more data while complying with the integrity constraints, as it would be the case for the prevented deletion anomalies. Indeed, in our example, the decomposed schema could store the salary of security guards even though there are no employees assigned to this position.

Decomposition is lossless if for any instance of the relation and the corresponding fragments the natural join of all the fragments is equal to the original relation. The following equation expresses this condition for the

Section 8.1. Anomalies and Decomposition

above example ($\bowtie_{natural}$ is the natural join):

$$employee = employee1 \bowtie_{natural} position$$

We recall that the expression above is equivalent to the following expression:

$$employee = \pi_{name,address,employee1.position,salary}$$
$$(employee1 \bowtie_{employee1.position=position.position} position)$$

Definition 8.2 *Let R be the scheme of a relation. Let S be a decomposition of R. We say that S is lossless if and only if for any instance $[R]$ of R (without anomaly):*

$$[R] = \bowtie_{natural(R_i \in S)} \pi_{R_i}([R])$$

Let us consider a new example. The relation *flight* has the following scheme:

$$flight(\quad flight\_number,$$
$$departure\_time,$$
$$arrival\_time,$$
$$origin, destination).$$

It is used to store basic flight information in the information system of a travel agent. It contains for recorded flights, the flight number, departure and arrival time, as well as the airport of origin and destination. An example instance of the *flight* relation is given in Figure 8.3. Let us assume, as it is the case in reality, that the flight number determines the departure time, arrival time, origin and destination.

flight_number	departure_time	arrival_time	origin	destination
SG012	12h00	13h00+	SIN	CDG
TG414	15h50	16h50	SIN	CGK
TG415	12h00	14h20	BKK	SIN

Figure 8.3: Flight Data

The decomposition illustrated in Figure 8.4 is lossy. It is not possible to recreate the relation instance in Figure 8.3 from the relation instances in Figure 8.4.

flight_number	departure_time	origin
SG012	12h00	SIN
TG414	15h50	SIN
TG415	12h00	BKK

departure_time	arrival_time	destination
12h00	13h00+	CDG
15h50	16h50	CGK
12h00	14h20	SIN

Figure 8.4: Lossy Decomposition of Flight Data

8.1.3 Dependency Preserving Decomposition

Decomposition may result in attributes that are related by a functional dependency that is scattered across several schemes. If such a situation occurs, we must make sure that the set of functional dependencies over individual tables in the decomposition is equivalent to the original set of functional dependencies. We must assume that the decomposition preserves the dependencies or is *dependency preserving*. For that purpose, we learn in Section 8.2 how to define and check the equivalence of two sets of functional dependencies. Then we give a formal definition of a dependency preserving decomposition.

8.1.4 Too Much Decomposition Harms

It might be tempting, following the above discussion, to decompose whenever it is possible in order to prevent anomalies. At this point, we must remember that decomposition induces more complex queries and hence less efficient processing. We must therefore, if possible, stop the decomposition as soon

Section 8.1. Anomalies and Decomposition

as the desired properties are enforced.

We can decompose the relation `flight` of Figure 8.3 into two, three or four tables such that the decomposition is lossless and dependency preserving. Figure 8.5 is an example of such a lossless dependency preserving decomposition in two tables. Yet, in this case, the decomposition is unnecessary to protect from anomalies and it would result in an extra cost for the evaluation of most queries since the fragments would have to be put together (join operation) to associate departure and origin with arrival and destination data. Even when decomposition is perfectly justifiable with respect to anomalies, we must also consider the typical workload of the application and decide on the trade-off between the risk of anomalies and specific efficiency requirements. In the subsequent section we present two normal forms, into one of which, at least, most database schemas are expected to be transformed. Yet, a designer is entitled not to produce schemas in these normal forms provided that she can justify her decision with respect to the workload. Furthermore, modern database management systems provide advanced tools for integrity maintenance (e.g. avoiding update anomalies) and other mechanisms that can reconcile normalisation and efficiency (e.g. materialised views).

flight_number	departure_time	origin
SG012	12h00	SIN
TG414	15h50	SIN
TG415	12h00	BKK

flight_number	arrival_time	destination
SG012	13h00+	CDG
TG414	16h50	CGK
TG415	14h20	SIN

Figure 8.5: Too Much Decomposition

8.2 Functional Dependencies

We have already discussed on many occasions the notion of functional dependency and we have given several intuitive definitions. In this section, we give a formal definition of a functional dependency and we study properties that we can use to reason about functional dependencies in order to perform an effective decomposition of relational schemas.

Definition 8.3 *Let R be the scheme of a relation. Let X and Y be two subsets of R. There is a functional dependency on R denoted $X \to Y$ if and only if, for every (valid) instance $[R]$ of R, if two t-uples agree on the values for the attributes in X then they agree on the values for the attributes in Y.*

All functional dependencies are not necessarily very interesting. Let us consider the following relation scheme:

$\quad employee(department\_name, location, manager, budget)$.

The following is a valid functional dependency:

$\quad \{department\_name\} \to \{department\_name\}$.

Both intuitively and formally we call such dependencies *trivial*.

Definition 8.4 *Let R be the scheme of a relation. Let X and Y be two subsets of R. Let $X \to Y$ be a functional dependency on R. $X \to Y$ is called trivial if and only if $Y \subset X$.*

Other dependencies are formally called *non-trivial*.

Definition 8.5 *Let R be the scheme of a relation. Let X and Y be two subsets of R. Let $X \to Y$ be a functional dependency on R. $X \to Y$ is called non-trivial if and only if $Y \not\subset X$.*

Yet, the presence of an attribute on both sides of a functional dependency intuitively does not carry non-trivial information. For instance, in the following functional dependency we can remove the attribute *manager* from the right hand side without any loss of information:

$$\{department\_name, manager\} \rightarrow \{location, manager\}.$$

Such functional dependencies are non-trivial according to the above definition, but, formally, we say that they are not *completely non-trivial*.

Definition 8.6 *Let R be the scheme of a relation. Let X and Y be two subsets of R. Let $X \rightarrow Y$ be a functional dependency on R. $X \rightarrow Y$ is called completely non-trivial if and only if $Y \cap X = \emptyset$.*

8.2.1 Keys

We have already discussed casually the relationship between functional dependencies and keys in conceptual and logical models. We can now give a series of formal definitions of the notions of key in the relational model. A key is a set of attributes in a relation scheme that determines all the attributes of the relation scheme. The fact that this set is minimum or not, and the choice that it is the one set that we designate to be the key, does differentiate a *candidate key*, from a *super-key*, from a *primary key*.

Definition 8.7 *Let R be the scheme of a relation. Let X be a subset of R. X is called a super-key, or simply a key, of R if and only if there exists a functional dependency $X \rightarrow R$ on R.*

Notice that R, i.e., the set of all attributes, is always a super-key, given that, in theory, a relation instance is a set.

Let us consider, for example, the following functional dependency on the relation *department* from the running example:

$$\{department\_name, manager\} \rightarrow$$
$$\{department\_name, location, manager, budget\}.$$

Remember that we have chosen *department_name* to be the key in the conceptual design and that the attribute *department_name* in the schema, as obtained after the translation of the Entity-Relationship diagram into a relational schema, is also chosen to be the primary key for the table `department` in SQL. This is possible because we know that departments have unique names. The set $\{department\_name, manager\}$ is a super-key according to our definition. Yet, the attribute *manager* seems unnecessary since the set $\{department\_name\}$ is also a super-key. We define a *candidate key* to be a minimal super-key.

Definition 8.8 *Let R be the scheme of a relation. Let X be a subset of R. X is called a candidate key of R if and only if there exists a functional dependency $X \rightarrow R$ on R and if $\forall Z \subset X, Z \neq X$, there does not exist a functional dependency $Z \rightarrow Y$.*

Definition 8.9 *Let R be the scheme of a relation. Let X be a candidate key of R. Elements in X are called prime attributes.*

There could be several candidate keys. Let us, for instance, consider a relation *customer* in a company's database application. The scheme of the relation, which is used to store information about customers of the company, such as, their name, address, national identification number and telephone number, is:

$$customer(name, address, national\_id\_num, telephone\_num).$$

Let us assume the following functional dependencies hold.

$$\{name, address\} \rightarrow$$
$$\{name, address, national\_id\_num, telephone\_num\}.$$

$$\{name, telephone\_num\} \rightarrow$$
$$\{name, address, national\_id\_num, telephone\_num\}.$$

$$\{national\_id\_num\} \rightarrow$$
$$\{name, address, national\_id\_num, telephone\_num\}.$$

The three sets of attributes $\{name, address\}$, $\{name, telephone\_num\}$ and $\{national\_id\_num\}$ are candidate keys. The designer arbitrarily chooses the *primary key* among the candidate keys.

Section 8.2. Functional Dependencies

Definition 8.10 *Let R be the scheme of a relation. Let X be a subset of R. X is called a primary key of R if and only if X is a candidate key designated by the designer.*

In SQL, the practical notion of primary key is slightly different from the one we define here. In SQL, a primary key is a super-key designated by the designer. It needs not be a candidate key, i.e., it needs not be a minimal set of attributes that constitutes a super-key. Most systems use the primary key information not only to control the consistency of the database and prevent duplicate insertion of t-uples with the same key, but also to build indices by hashing the values of the attributes in the key to optimise access to data (assuming that data is mainly accessed through its key) and to facilitate the maintenance of integrity (it is faster to check for duplicate entries with such an index). This logic obviously originates from the technology and could be reconsidered if the necessary technological development occurred. In particular, it should be sufficient to indicate a complete set of functional dependencies and let the system determine the candidate keys, choose the primary keys and maintain consistency and efficiency.

Notice that the term *key* alone sometimes refer to super-key, candidate key or primary key depending on authors and textbooks. We shall try to be explicit.

8.2.2 Reasoning about Functional Dependencies

The designer of a database application may have only identified some of the functional dependencies holding on each scheme in the schema of the database. This might be the case (and probably is the case), even though she has managed to capture all the knowledge about functional dependencies. Indeed, many functional dependencies can be deduced from those identified. Before proceeding to the decomposition and normalisation of the schemes, we need to present the tools that can help us to reason about functional dependencies: to compare them, find all the consequences of a set of functional dependencies or minimise sets of functional dependencies and functional dependencies themselves.

Simple reasoning about functional dependencies might be intuitive. For instance, it may seem obvious to some that the functional dependency:

$$\{department\_name, manager\} \rightarrow \{manager, budget\}$$

is equivalent to the functional dependency:

$$\{department\_name, manager\} \rightarrow \{budget\}.$$

The reader is invited to attempt to write the proof starting from the definition of a functional dependency. It would be more convenient to reason with a sound and complete system of inference rules to derive all correct functional dependencies from a set of known functional dependencies. Fortunately, such systems of inference rules exist. The Armstrong's axioms constitute such a system.

Definition 8.11 *Let R be the scheme of a relation. Let X, Y and Z be subsets of R. The following three rules are called Armstrong's axioms and are named reflexivity, augmentation and transitivity, respectively.*

Reflexivity: *If $Y \subset X$ then $X \rightarrow Y$;*

Augmentation: *If $X \rightarrow Y$ then $X \cup Z \rightarrow Y \cup Z$;*

Transitivity: *If $X \rightarrow Y$ and $Y \rightarrow Z$ then $X \rightarrow Z$.*

Property 8.1 *The Armstrong's axioms are sound.*

Although we omit the proof of this property, it is rather intuitive that each inference made using each of the three axioms is correct given the definition of a functional dependency. In other words, given a set of functional dependencies on a relation scheme, the new functional dependencies that we can deduce using the Armstrong's axioms are functional dependencies on the relation scheme.

Property 8.2 *The Armstrong's axioms are complete.*

We omit the proof again. This result is much more powerful and surprising. Indeed, completeness tells us that, given a set of functional dependencies on a relation scheme, we can deduce all the functional dependencies

Section 8.2. Functional Dependencies

that hold on the relation scheme using the Armstrong's axioms. The proof of completeness is not as simple as the proof of soundness.

Thanks to soundness and completeness, we have with the Armstrong's axioms a tool for reasoning about functional dependencies.

For a given set of functional dependencies, the set of all the functional dependencies that can be deduced by applying the Armstrong's axioms (or any other sound and complete set of inference rules) is called the closure.

Definition 8.12 *Let R be the scheme of a relation. Let F be a set of functional dependencies on R. We call the closure of F denoted F^+ the set of functional dependencies entailed by the dependencies in F.*

The notion of closure gives us the opportunity to define the equivalence of sets of functional dependencies. Indeed, if two sets of functional dependencies have the same closure, they implicitly capture the same information about the scheme. Therefore, they are called equivalent.

Definition 8.13 *Let R be the scheme of a relation. Let F and G be two sets of functional dependencies on R. We say that F and G are equivalent if and only if:*

$$F^+ = G^+.$$

The above definition suggests a naïve algorithm for the test of equivalence. This algorithm computes both closures and tests their equality as outlined in Figure 8.6.

Let us introduce the notion of closure for a set of attributes. We use this notion to devise a better algorithm for testing the equivalence of two sets of functional dependencies.

Definition 8.14 *Let R be the scheme of a relation and F a set of functional dependencies on R. Let $X \subset R$. We call $Y \subset R$, denoted $X^{+(F)}$ (or X^+ if there is no ambiguity), the closure of X with respect to F, the largest set of attributes of R such that $X \to Y$ is entailed by F.*

The algorithm outlined in Figure 8.7 computes the closure of a set of attributes with respect to a set of functional dependencies. Starting from the initial set of attributes, the algorithm iteratively applies all functional dependencies as production rules until no new attribute is added to the set.

```
Let R be a relation scheme
Let F and G be sets of functional dependencies on R
begin
compute F⁺
compute G⁺
if F⁺ = G⁺
    then return F is equivalent to G
    else return F is not equivalent to G;
end
```

Figure 8.6: Naïve Algorithm for Testing the Equivalence of Two Sets of Functional Dependencies

```
Let R be a relation scheme
Let X ⊂ R
Let F be a set of functional dependencies on R
begin
i = 0;
X⁽ⁱ⁾ = X;
repeat
    i = i + 1;
    X⁽ⁱ⁾ = ⋃₍Y⊂X⁽ⁱ⁻¹⁾₎∧₍₍Y→Z₎∈F₎ Z;
until X⁽ⁱ⁾ = X⁽ⁱ⁻¹⁾
return X⁽ⁱ⁾;
end
```

Figure 8.7: Algorithm for Computing the Closure of a Set of Attributes with Respect to a Set of Functional Dependencies

Section 8.2. Functional Dependencies

We can now devise a new algorithm for the test of equivalence of two sets of functional dependencies leveraging the notion of attribute closure. The new algorithm, depicted in Figure 8.8, tests that each functional dependency in one set is entailed by the other set. Indeed, a functional dependency $(X \rightarrow Y)$ is entailed by a set of functional dependencies F if and only if $Y \subset X^{+(F)}$.

```
Let R be a relation scheme
Let F and G be sets of functional dependencies on R
begin
    for each (X → Y) ∈ F
        compute X+(G);
        if Y ⊄ X+(G)
            then the sets are not equivalent;
    endfor

    for each (X → Y) ∈ G
        compute X+(F);
        if Y ⊄ X+(F)
            then return F is not equivalent to G; exit;
    endfor
    return F is equivalent to G;
end
```

Figure 8.8: Algorithm for Testing the Equivalence of Two Sets of Functional Dependencies

We are now trying to define the notion of a minimal set of functional dependencies. This set of functional dependencies, as indicated by its name, must be minimal and somehow in a canonical form.

In order to motivate the notion of minimality, let us consider the following sets of functional dependencies.

$$F = \{\{A\} \rightarrow \{B, C, D\}\}.$$

$$G = \{\{A\} \to \{B\}, \{A\} \to \{C, D\}\}.$$

$$H = \{\{A\} \to \{B\}, \{A\} \to \{C\}, \{A\} \to \{D\}\}.$$

Clearly the three sets are equivalent. Using the Armstrong's axioms the reader can verify that both the following inference rules are sound for R the scheme of a relation, and X, Y and Z subsets of R:

$$If\ X \to Y \cup Z\ then\ X \to Y\ and\ X \to Z,$$

$$If\ X \to Y\ and\ X \to Z\ then\ X \to Y \cup Z.$$

Let us arbitrarily agree to prefer H as a canonical representation of constraints. By convention, in a minimal set of functional dependencies, functional dependencies have a singleton on the right hand side.

Let us also consider the following sets of functional dependencies.

$$F = \{\{A, E\} \to \{C\}, \{B\} \to \{D\}, \{D\} \to \{C\}\}.$$

$$G = \{\{A, B, E\} \to \{C\}, \{B\} \to \{D\}, \{D\} \to \{C\}\}.$$

One can verify that F and G are equivalent. Yet, the first constraint of F is similar to the first constraint of G to the left hand side of which the attribute B has been removed. We prefer F as it represents the same information more concisely. In a minimal set of functional dependencies, functional dependencies have a left hand side that is minimal for inclusion.

Finally, if two sets F and G of functional dependencies are equivalent and such that $F \subset G$, we shall prefer F as it represents the same information more concisely. A minimal set of functional dependencies is minimal for inclusion.

Definition 8.15 *Let R be the scheme of a relation. Let F be a set of functional dependencies on R. We say that F is minimal if and only if $\forall (X \to Y) \in F$:*

1. *Y is a singleton;*

2. *$\forall Z \subset X, Z \neq X, (F - \{X \to Y\}) \cup \{Z \to Y\}$ is not equivalent to F;*

Section 8.2. Functional Dependencies

3. $F - \{X \to Y\}$ is not equivalent to F.

We can now define the *minimal cover* of a set of functional dependencies.

Definition 8.16 *Let F be a set of functional dependencies. A minimal set of functional dependencies equivalent to F is called a minimal cover of F.*

A given set of functional dependencies may have several minimal covers. Indeed, since inclusion confers only a partial order on sets, uniqueness is not guaranteed. There may be several minimal sets of functional dependencies equivalent to a given set of functional dependencies. However, we claim but do not prove that every set of functional dependencies has a minimal cover.

The first requirement can be enforced by applying the inference rule discussed above:

$If\ X \to Y \cup Z\ then\ X \to Y\ and\ X \to Z.$

Equivalent sets of functional dependencies that meet the second and third requirements are equally easy to obtain. If there exists a functional dependency $X \to Y$ such that there exists $Z \subset X, Z \neq X$, and $(F - \{X \to Y\}) \cup \{Z \to Y\}$ is equivalent to F, then replace it with $Z \to Y$. If there is a functional dependency $X \to Y$ such that $F - \{X \to Y\}$ is equivalent to F, then remove it.

An obvious algorithm to compute a minimal set of functional dependencies equivalent to a set of functional dependencies F consists of iteratively transforming the set F according to the three transformations described, trying at each step to enforce one of the three properties given in the definition until the transformed set verifies the three properties of the definition.

A strong and unexpected result, which we do not prove here, tells us that it suffices to apply the first transformation for all the functional dependencies in F, then the second transformation for all the functional dependencies in the resulting set, then the third transformation for all the functional dependencies in the resulting set without iterations to compute the minimal cover of F. Figure 8.9 summarises the algorithm.

If, for the sake of concision, we prefer to maximise the right hand side of functional dependencies, and therefore reduce their number, e.g. if we

```
Let R be a relation scheme
Let F be a set of functional dependencies on R
begin
   (1) transform each right hand side
       of functional dependencies into a singleton;
   (2) For each functional dependency X → Y
       If ∃Z ⊂ X, Z ≠ X such that
       (F − {X → Y}) ∪ {Z → Y} is equivalent to F
       then replace X → Y with Z → Y;
   (3) For each functional dependency X → Y such that
       (F − {X → Y}) is equivalent to F
       then remove X → Y;
   return F;
end
```

Figure 8.9: Minimal Cover Algorithm

preferred the set $\{X \to Y \cup Z\}$ over the set $\{X \to Y, X \to Z\}$, we shall call the thus obtained set the *extended minimal cover*.

8.2.3 Dependency Preserving Decomposition

We first need to define the notion of projection of a set of functional dependencies on the scheme of a relation. This notion helps us recover all the proper functional dependencies on the fragments of the decomposed relation. Notice in the definition that we use the closure of the set of functional dependencies and not the original set itself.

Definition 8.17 *Let R be the scheme of a relation, and F a set of functional dependencies (notice that F may involve attributes not in R). F_R is a projection of F on R if and only if*

$$\forall (X \to Y) \in F_R \ (X \subset R) \text{ and } (Y \subset R) \text{ and } (X \to Y) \in F^+$$

and

$$\forall (X \to Y) \in F^+ \ ((X \subset R) \ and \ (Y \subset R)) \implies (X \to Y) \in F_R{}^+$$

Some authors speak about *the projection* of F on R (instead of *a projection*) sometimes referring to $F_R{}^+$.

The decomposition of the scheme of a relation is dependency preserving if the union of the projections of the original set of functional dependencies on the fragments is equivalent to the original set of functional dependencies.

Definition 8.18 *Let R be the scheme of a relation. Let S be a set of relational schemes R_i and a decomposition of R. Let F be the set of functional dependencies associated with the scheme R, and F_i projections of F according to R_i, respectively. We call S a dependency preserving decomposition if and only if*

$$(\bigcup_i F_i)^+ = F^+.$$

8.3 Normalisation

We recall here that a database schema is in first normal form or 1NF if the domains of the attributes are scalar, i.e., the domains contain values that are not complex values such as relations, lists, sets or t-uples. In most of this text, we have assumed that a relational schema is always in 1NF. The first normal form imposes some structural constraints.

The second, third and Boyce-Codd normal forms define conditions based on functional dependencies under which relation schemes or relational schemas have good properties with regard to anomalies. In the rest of this section we focus on third and Boyce-Codd normal forms. The second normal form is presented for historical reasons. We give algorithms to decompose the scheme of a relation into 3NF and BCNF, respectively.

In the second normal form, non-prime attributes (a prime attribute is an attribute that belongs to a candidate key) cannot be functionally dependent on a subset of a candidate key.

Definition 8.19 *Let R be a relation scheme, and F the associated set of functional dependencies. R is in second normal form or 2NF if and only if $\forall (X \to \{A\}) \in F^+$:*

- *$A \in X$ (i.e., the functional dependency is trivial), or*

- *X is not a proper subset[1] of any candidate key for R or*

- *A is an element of some candidate key for R (i.e., A is a prime attribute).*

In Boyce-Codd normal form, each attribute can only be non-trivially functionally dependent upon a super-key.

Definition 8.20 *Let R be a relation scheme, and F the associated set of functional dependencies, R is in Boyce-Codd normal form or BCNF if and only if $\forall (X \to \{A\}) \in F^+$*

- *$A \in X$ (i.e., the functional dependency is trivial) or*

- *X is a super-key for R.*

We claim and do not prove that every relational scheme has a lossless decomposition into BCNF.

Figure 8.10 outlines an algorithm for computing the lossless decomposition of a relation scheme into a BCNF schema. Whenever a functional dependency $X \to \{Y\}$ (with a singleton right hand side) violates the BCNF condition for a scheme R, the scheme is decomposed according to the set X into two schemes: $(R - X^+) \cup X$ and X^+. A projection of the set of functional dependencies on each fragment must be considered at each iteration. We claim and do not prove the soundness and completeness of the algorithm.

Since the only non-trivial dependencies in a BCNF correspond to superkeys, a BCNF is safe from anomalies caused by embedded dependencies. However, it may be the case that no BCNF decomposition exists that is dependency preserving. For such cases, the third normal form is available.

---

[1] A set S_1 is a proper subset of a set S_2 if and only if S_1 is a subset of S_2, $S_1 \subset S_2$, and the two sets are different, $S_1 \neq S_2$.

Section 8.3. Normalisation

```
    Let R be a relation scheme
    Let F be a set of functional dependencies on R
      S = {R};
      For each fragment T ∈ S
      compute a projection F_T of F on T
      While some fragment T ∈ S is not in BCNF
         since T is not in BCNF
             ∃X → {Y} ∈ F_T^+
             such that X → R does not hold and
             Y ∉ X
         let S be (S − T) ∪ {(T − X^+) ∪ X, X^+}
      endwhile
    return S;
    end
```

Figure 8.10: Algorithm for the Decomposition of a Relational Schema into BCNF

In third normal form, non-prime attributes can only be non-trivially functionally dependent upon a super-key.

Definition 8.21 *Let R be a relation scheme, and F the associated set of functional dependencies. R is in third normal form or 3NF if and only if $\forall (X \to \{A\}) \in F^+$*

- *$A \in X$ (i.e., the functional dependency is trivial) or*

- *X is a super-key for R, or*

- *A is part of some candidate key for R (i.e., A is a prime attribute).*

We claim and do not prove that every relational scheme has a lossless decomposition into 3NF.

Figure 8.11 outlines an algorithm for computing a lossless decomposition of a relation scheme into a 3NF schema. We claim and do not prove the completeness and correctness of the algorithm. We also claim without proof that a decomposition obtained with this algorithm is always dependency preserving. However, unlike BCNF decompositions, some redundancy can be detected in 3NF decompositions.

```
Let R be a relation scheme
Let F be a set of functional dependencies on R

Compute $F^{min}$ an extended minimal cover of F

$S = \emptyset$;
for each functional dependency $(X \to Y) \in F^{min}$
    if no scheme in S contains $X \cup Y$
    then create a new relation with scheme $X \cup Y$
endfor

if no scheme contains a candidate key for R
then create a scheme with a candidate key for R
    add it to $S$
return $S$;
end
```

Figure 8.11: Algorithm for the Synthesis of a Relation Scheme into 3NF

The strategy we propose for the 3NF decomposition algorithm is fundamentally different from the one for the BCNF algorithm. While the BCNF algorithm decomposes the scheme into fragments using the functional dependencies, the 3NF algorithm composes fragments from the functional dependencies. This algorithm is often referred to as 3NF *synthesis*. There exist other decomposition algorithms for 3NF.

For both the decomposition into BCNF and the synthesis into 3NF, the algorithms leave choices to the programmer. For instance, the programmer has to choose which minimal cover is computed and used in the 3NF decomposition. There might indeed be several valid BCNF and 3NF decompositions of a given relation scheme.

It is also easy, from the definitions, to see that the set of relational schemas in Boyce-Codd normal form is necessarily in third normal form, the set of relational schemas in third normal form is in second normal form, and that the set of relational schemas in second normal form is in first normal form. In practice, it also seems that most relational schemas in 3NF are in BCNF.

In summary, we can say that normalisation should aim at a lossless and dependency preserving BCNF decomposition. If such decomposition is not possible, then a 3NF lossless and dependency preserving decomposition should be sought.

There exist other normal forms, in particular normal forms that seek to avoid anomalies related to other kinds of integrity constraints than functional dependencies. For instance, the fourth normal form is defined with respect to multi-valued dependencies. Database designers usually normalise their schema in BCNF or 3NF unless the protection against other anomalies is critically required by the application.

Chapter 9

Conclusion

"Tout sera oublié et rien ne sera réparé ; le rôle de la réparation sera tenu par l'oubli."[1]

M. Kundera, *La Plaisanterie*

9.1 Further Readings

There are literally tens of thousands of textbooks on database applications design and programming and on the practice and theory of database management systems. This text does not intend to be yet another book on database but rather tries and presents fundamental concepts and techniques for the design and implementation of database applications with a relational database management system. To this extent, it compels further readings.

In the field of databases, which has been and continues to be developing under the mutual influence of practitioners and theoreticians, there is little consensus about the vocabulary and the notations. Sometimes even the concepts are still being discussed. It is therefore necessary, in order to develop an understanding of the concepts underlying the design and implementation of databases, to read several works and critically compare their presentation of each topic. Only such an approach can build a knowledge that survives the trends and the idiosyncrasies of specific commercial data management systems.

This book is intended to be a guideline and a reference for the reader studying design and querying in relational database management systems. It has been written assuming that the reader has at hand at least another database textbook rich in detailed discussions, examples, and exercises, for instance, one of the following four textbooks:

---

[1] Everything will be forgotten. There will never be any redress for anything.

- *Database Management Systems* (Ramakrishnan and Gehrke, 2003);

- *Database Systems Concepts* (Silberschatz and Korth, 1997);

- *Database Systems, Concepts, Languages and Architecture* (Atzeni, Ceri, Paraboschi and Torlone, 1999);

- *A First Course in Database Systems* (Ullman and Widom, 2002).

Each of the above presents and discusses additional topics not covered in this book. In particular, the first three also cover issues related to the architecture of database management systems. The authors of the latter, together with Hector Garcia-Molina, have written a second book, *Database Systems Implementation* (Ullman et al., 2000) which discusses the architecture and implementation of database management systems. The two books by these authors have been combined into a single volume: *Database Systems, the Complete Book* (Ullman et al., 2002).

The classic reference and probably the most widely used by university students and lecturers around the world is *An Introduction to Database Systems* (Date, 2004).

We also suggest both *Relational Database Systems* (Adiba and Delobel, 1985) and *Relational Databases and Knowledge Bases* (Gardarin and Valduriez, 1989) as rich sources of examples and exercises.

The Theory of Relational Database (Maier, 1983) is a complete reference on the relational model, relational algebra, relational calculus, as well as on normalisation.

The graphical notations for the Entity-Relationship diagrams we use in this book follow those introduced in *Conceptual Database Design, an Entity-Relationship Approach* (Batini, Ceri and Navathe, 1992). The book comprehensively discusses the design of database applications with the Entity-Relationship model.

For the graduate student in computer science and the reader intending to pursue a career as a database researcher or as designer of database software, must-read and necessary handbooks are the two volumes of *Data and Knowledge-Base Systems* (Ullman, 1988). For both researchers and practitioners, *Database Tuning* (Shasha and Bonnet, 2003) is the practical guide to the management of performance for database applications.

Finally, a comprehensive collection of seminal research papers is available in *Readings in Database Systems* (Stonebraker and Hellerstein, 1998). It contains, in particular, reprints of two articles "A Relational Model for Large Shared Data Banks" and "The Entity-relationship Model: Toward a Unified View of Data".

References

Adiba, M. and Delobel, C. (1985). *Relational Database Systems.* Elsevier Science, Amsterdam, Holland.

Atzeni, P., Ceri, S., Paraboschi, S. and Torlone, R. (1999). *Database Systems, Concepts, Languages and Architecture.* McGraw-Hill, Maidenhead, Berkshire, England.

Batini, C., Ceri, S. and Navathe, S. B. (1992). *Conceptual Database Design, an Entity Relationship Approach.* Benjamin Cummings, Redwood City, CA.

Date, C. (2004). *An Introduction to Database Systems.* (8th edition). Addison-Wesley, Boston, MA.

Gardarin, G. and Valduriez, P. (1989). *Relational Databases and Knowledge Bases.* Addison-Wesley, Reading, MA.

Maier, D. (1983). *The Theory of Relational Databases.* Computer Science Press, Inc., Rockville, MD.

Ramakrishnan, R. and Gehrke, J. (2003). *Database Management Systems.* (3rd edition). McGraw-Hill, New York, NY.

Shasha, D. and Bonnet, P. (2003). *Database Tuning.* Morgan Kaufmann, San Francisco, CA.

Silberschatz, A. and Korth, H. F. (1997). *Database Systems Concepts.* (4th edition). McGraw-Hill, Boston, MA.

Stonebraker, M. and Hellerstein, J. (1998). *Readings in Database Systems.* (4th edition). Morgan Kaufmann, Cambridge, MA.

Ullman, J. (1988). *Principles of Database and Knowledge-Base Systems.* Computer Science Press, Inc., Rockville, MD.

Ullman, J. D. and Widom, J. (2002). *A First Course in Database Systems.* (2nd edition). Prentice Hall, Inc., Upper Saddle River, NJ.

Ullman, J. D., Widom, J. and Garcia-Molina, H. (2000). *Database Systems Implementation.* Prentice Hall, Inc., Upper Saddle River, NJ.

Ullman, J. D., Widom, J. and Garcia-Molina, H. (2002). *Database Systems, the Complete Book.* Prentice Hall, Inc., Upper Saddle River, NJ.

Index

The letter f followed by page numbers indicates figures.

θ-condition, 41, 45, 65
θ-join operator, 45

Access
    Access control, 5
    Access rights, 3, 51
ACID properties, 2–3
    Atomicity, 2
    Consistency, 2–3
    Durability, 2, 3
    Isolation, 2, 3
Aggregate functions, 67–68
    AVG function, 67
    COUNT function, 67
    MAX function, 67
    MIN function, 67
    SUM function, 67
Aggregate queries, 67–69
Algebra, *see* Relational algebra
Aliases, 64
Anomalies, 123–125, f124, 145
    Deletion anomalies, 124–125
    Insertion anomalies, 125
    Redundant storage anomalies, 124
    Update anomalies, 124
Application designers, 4, 7
Application programmers, 4, 6, 7
Armstrong's axioms, 134–135, 138
    Augmentation, 134
    Reflexivity, 134
    Transitivity, 134
Assertions, 56–57, 59
Atomic values, 10, 16
Attributes, 10, 11

BCNF, *see* Boyce-Codd normal form
Boyce-Codd normal form (BCNF), 123, 141, 142, 144–145
    Algorithm for the decomposition into, 142, f143, 144

Cardinality
    Constraints, 120
    Maximum participation of, 116
    Minimum participation of, 116
    Of a relation, 11
Cartesian product, 11, 106
Cartesian product operator, 43, f44
Chen, P., 105
Composability property, 37
Computational completeness, 73
Conceptual model, 7, 105, 131
Concurrency control, 2, 5
Concurrent access, 2
Conjunction, 19, f21, 24, 31, 45

Connectives, 19, 20, 22, 24, 28, 29, 31, 35
Constraints, 110–117, 118
   see also Integrity constraints
Correlation names, see Aliases
Cursor, 76, 80, 81, 100

Database administrator, 4, 6, 7
Database application, 2, 3
Database connectivity, 75, 86–87
   Reference architecture, 87–89, f89
Database control language (DCL), 4, 51
Database design, 5–6
Database instances, 37
Database management system (DBMS), 3–8, 49, 51, 74, 75, 123, 147
   Components of, 4, f5
   Data in, 5, f6
   End-users, 4
Database tuning, 7, 118, 123
Data definition language (DDL), 4, 51, 52–60
Data manipulation language (DML), 4, 51, 60–72
   Data model, 2, 7–8
DBMS, see Database management system
DCL, see Database control language
DDL, see Data definition language
Declarativeness of query language, 48–49

Decompositions, 14, 125, f126, f128, f129
   Dependency preserving decompositions, 128, 140–141, 144–145, f144
   Fragments, 126
   Lossless decompositions, 125–128, 142–145, f143, f144
Default values, 53, 78
Disjunction, 19, f21, 24, 31, 35
Distributed access, 2
DML, see Data manipulation language
Domain, 10, 13
Domain relational calculus, 19, 28–34, 35, 48
Dominant entities, 114–115, 116
Dot notation, 46, 63

E. F. Codd, 9
Embedded SQL, 75, 97
Entities, 105–122, f106, f107, f108, f110, f112, f119
Entity-relationship diagram, 105–122, f115
   Translation to relational schema, 117–122
Entity-relationship model, 105–122
Equijoin, 45
Exception handling, 77, 95
   System exceptions, 82
   User exception, 82
Existentially quantified formula, 24–25, 31

Exists, 71
Expression, 22
Extended minimal cover, 139
External algorithms, 2
    External sort, 2
External coupling, 74
    Connection, 89–90

First normal form (1NF), 10, 141
First order logic, 19, 20–21
Foreign key constraint, 16, 53
Formulae
    Atomic formulae, 22
    Complex formulae, 22
    In domain relational calculus, 19, 28–30
    In t-uple relational calculus, 19, 21–22
    Well-formed formulae, 22, 23
Functional dependencies, 15, 128, 130–131, 133, 134, 137, 138
    Closure of a set of, 135, $f136$
    Equivalent sets of, 135, $f136$, 137, $f137$, $f138$, 139
    Minimal cover of a set of, 137, 138, 139–140

Generalised dependencies, 15, 17, 53
Ground term, 31

Homogeneous collections, 2

Implication, 20, $f21$, 35
Inclusion dependencies, 15, 16

Inner-join, 45
Instance
    Relation instance 11, 37
    Of the schema, 13
Integrity constraints, 3, 14–17, 117, 122, 123, 125, 126, 145
    In SQL, 53–57
Internal coupling, 74
Intersection operator, 37, 39, $f40$
Invoked routines, 83

$Java^{TM}$, 99, 100, 102
$JDBC^{TM}$, 89, 94, 95, 99
Join operator, 43–45, $f45$

Key, 15, 111, $f111$, 112, 131, 133
    Candidate key, 132
    Composite key, 111, $f112$
    Foreign key, 16, 53, 120
    Primary key, 15, 16, 53–54, 132–133
    Of a relation, 15
    Super-key, 131
    Key constraints, 111, 118
Knowledge independence, 7, 59

Logical data independence, 6–7, $f7$, 59
Logical data model, 6, 8

Mandatory or total participation in a relationship, 113, 121
Many-to-many relationship, 114
Metadata, 5

Minimal cover, 139
    Algorithm, f140
Model, 105
Multi-valued dependencies, 15, 16

Natural join, 45
Negation, 20, f21, 35
Nested queries, 69–70, 71, 72
    see also Sub-queries
Network model, 8
NF2, see Non first normal form
Non first normal form (NF2), 10
Non-symmetrical difference operator, 37, 40, f40
Non-trivial dependencies, 130–131
Normalisation, 123, 145
Not null constraints, 15, 17, 53, 54, 78
Null values, 13–14, 15, 93

Object-oriented model, 8, 105
1NF, see First normal form
One-to-many relationship, 114, 122
One-to-one relationship, 114
Optional or partial participation in a relationship, 113
Oracle 9i^{TM}, 101
Outer-join, 45

Participation constraints, 111, 113–114, f113, f114, 116, 118
Physical data independence, 6, 8
Physical data model, 6

PL/SQL^{TM}, 78, 79, 80, 82, 83, 84, 85
Procedural SQL, 77–86
Programming languages, 74
Projection attribute, 42
Projection operator, 42, f42
Propositional logic, 19–20, 24, 31

Queries
    In domain relational calculus, 33–34, 34–35
    Project-Select-Join (PSJ) queries, 65
    In relational algebra, 37, 46–48
    In SQL, see SQL queries
    In t-uple relational calculus, 26–27, 34–35
Query language, 6, 19, 37, 51

Recovery, 2, 5
Reference to attribute, 71
Referential integrity constraints, 16, 53, 54, 55, 57–58, 118, 120
Relation, 9, f9, 11
    Arity or degree, 11
    Cardinality, 11
    Instance, 11, 37
    Schema, 11
    Scheme, 11
Relational algebra, 37–49 f48
    Set operators, 37
Relational calculus
    Domain, 19

Index 157

T-uple, 19, 22
Relational model, 8, 10, 65, 105
Relationships, 105–122, *f*107, *f*108, *f*110, *f*112, *f*119
    Binary relationships, 108, 109
    Ternary relationships, 108, 109, *f*109
    Unary relationships, 108
Renaming operator, 45–46
Roll back, 2, 95

Safe query, 35, 48
Schema of a relation, *see* Relation: Schema
Scrollability, 93
Second normal form, 141–142
Selection operator, 41, *f*41
Semantics
    Domain relational calculus, 19, 30–33
    T-uple relational calculus, 19, 23–27
SQL, *see* Structured Query Language
SQL clauses
    FROM clause, 62
    GROUP clause, 68
    HAVING clause, 66, 69
    SELECT clause, 62, 65, 68
    WHERE clause, 53, 62, 63, 69
SQL constraints
    CHECK, 55–56, 57
    Not null, 15, 17, 53, 54, 78
    Primary ley, 15, 16, 53, 54
    References, 54–55

    Unique, 15, 17, 53, 54
SQLj, 97, 99, 100, 101
SQL-99, 73, 77, 83, 85, 87
SQL-92, 73
SQL queries, 62, 63, 65–66, 69
    Aggregate queries, 67
    Nested queries, 62–63
    Simple queries, 69–70, 71, 72
SQL statements, 51, 75, 77, 78, 79, 91, 92, 97, 98, 99
    ALTER TABLE, 59
    CREATE ASSERTION, 56
    CREATE TABLE, 52, 53
    CREATE VIEW, 58
    DELETE TABLE, 61, 91
    DROP TABLE, 59
    INSERT, 60, 91
    SELECT, 62, 63, 64, 65, 66, 68, 80, 91
    UPDATE, 61, 91
Statements
    CLOSE, 81
    Collection of results, 75
    Dynamic statements, 75, 76, 82
    Execution of, 75
    Non-prepared statements, 90
    OPEN, 80
    Preparation of, 75
    Prepared statements, 90, 92
    Static statements, 75–76
    see also SQL statements
State of the database, 13, 15
Stored functions, 83, 85

Stored procedures, 83, 84
Strings in SQL, 60, 90–91
Structured data, 2
Structured Query Language (SQL), 8, 51–72, 73, 74, 133
    Procedural extension of, 77–86
Sub-queries, 69, 70, 71
    see also Nested queries
Syntax
    Domain relational calculus, 28–30
    T-uple relational calculus, 21–23
System completeness (also resource completeness), 74

Tables, 55, 59, 65, 69
Third normal form, 123, 141, 142, 143–145
    Algorithm for the synthesis into, 143, f144
3NF, see Third normal form
Transactions, 2, 15, 57, 62, 82
Trivial dependencies, 130
T-uple relational calculus, 19, 20–28, 35, 48
T-uples, 11, 16, 62, 80

2NF, see Second normal form

Union compatibility, 39
Union operator, 37, 38, f39
Unique constraints, 15, 17, 53, 54, 121
Universally quantified formula, 24, 31
Unsafe query, 35

Values, 22, 24, 25, 28, 31, 93
Variables, 28, 30
    In domain relational calculus, 33
    Existentially quantified variables, 27, 33
    Free, 23, 26, 27, 30, 32, 33
    Quantified variables, 24, 27, 31, 33
    In t-uple relational calculus, 27
Views, 7, 58–59
View update problem, 59

Weak entities, 114–117, f116, f117, 121
Weak key or weak identification, 117